D1377812

Instant Asia

Joseph Grima

Instant Asia

Fast Forward through the Architecture of a Changing Continent

photographs by
Gaia Cambiaggi

Editor
Luca Molinari

Design
Marcello Francone

Editorial Coordination
Emma Cavazzini

Editing
Emanuela Di Lallo

Layout
Sara Salvi

Editorial Assistant
Jessica Russell

Photographic Credits
Gaia Cambiaggi for all the photographs
Photographs pp. 120–21, 123–27
courtesy Mass Studies

First published in Italy in 2008
by Skira Editore S.p.A.
Palazzo Casati Stampa
via Torino 61
20123 Milano
Italy
www.skira.net

Printed and bound in Italy. First edition

ISBN: 978-88-6130-303-4

Distributed in North America by Rizzoli International Publications, Inc., 300 Park Avenue South, New York, NY 10010, USA.
Distributed elsewhere in the world by Thames and Hudson Ltd., 181A High Holborn, London WC1V 7QX, United Kingdom.

Thank you to Luca Molinari, for his unfailing support, invaluable advice and longsuffering patience; Takaharu and Yui Tezuka, for their remarkable generosity, their hospitality and for numerous introductions and logistic support in Tokyo; Minsuk Cho, for his irrepressible enthusiasm and for instantly connecting us to Seoul; Qingyun Ma, for his numerous introductions in China and his invaluable advice; Rachaporn Choochuey, Stefano Mirti and Kayoko Ota, for their suggestions and introductions; Takashi Yamasaki, Masato Ikuta and Aya Fukamoto, our guides in Tokyo; Abel Segretin and Jeremie Descamps for their hospitality; Maki Nanamori and SangHoon Lee for translating and accompanying us; Paolo Cecchetto for the Italian translation of this book; the copy editor and graphic designer of Skira, for their commitment and dedication to this book; Stefano Boeri, for his unwavering encouragement and counsel.

Contents

Asia Now: A Polaroid of a Changing Continent

Joseph Grima

This book is a snapshot, a collection of fragments, a sequence of situations. Like a burst of frames fired by a photojournalist who has the good fortune of witnessing a fleeting moment of action that will later come to define an era, it is an attempt to synchronically document a complex phenomenon by capturing its essence rather than describing its entirety – *pars pro toto*. For this reason it is unavoidably subjective, incomplete and even reductive. How can one accurately describe the velocity, complexity and vigour of a struggle – especially if it is not yet over and the outcome is still uncertain – without stepping, even briefly, into its epicentre?

As the media tirelessly remind us, Asian cities are the locus of a revolution that for well over a decade has been progressively and exponentially changing the face of the continent. This metamorphosis is part of a broader wave of changes that have affected Asian societies in a multitude of ways: in a stunningly brief period of time agricultural economies have become industrial economies, industrial economies have transmuted into post-industrial economies, democracies have replaced dictatorships, and millions of people have achieved previously unimaginable wealth. As we all know, these changes have not always been for the better, and have almost always come at a cost: wealth has entailed widespread social disenfranchisement and segregation, industrial development has come at the expense of rampant exploitation, and urbanisation has frequently been synonymous with 'slumification'.

Since these changes have most visibly impacted Asia's urban centres, architects have found themselves the involuntary midwives of a painful delivery that is as yet far from over. Motivated to take action by their instincts of survival, architects – and consequently architecture – have been forced to reflect, react and evolve. More than works of architecture, this book documents an unfinished process of evolution, using built works as litmus papers to gauge and investigate the surrounding conditions. Situations of crisis brought about by rapid and unexpected change are often the most fertile context for the birth of new ideas, but there is a lag time between action and reaction. Perhaps now, for the first time, it is possible to make a reading of the ideas, positions and solutions emerging from this complex and dynamic scenario. Particularly in the case of China and South Korea, the new-found prosperity of recent decades caused a rapid increase in the number of students travelling abroad to the US and Europe, and those students have now returned, founded practices and implemented a process of negotiation and reinterpretation of these multiple cultural influences and contexts. Even as short a time as five years ago, such an analysis would have been speculative; today it is possible to tentatively investigate how the new generation of architects are coming to terms with, and gradually learning to creatively respond to alterations in the reality that surrounds them.

This isn't a biography of contemporary architecture in Asia – if anything it is a portrait, assembled through fragments, of a specific instant in time. As with any portrait, as much of the information it contains is implicit as explicit. Such is the complexity of the forces at play that only a piecemeal understanding of the phenomena driving these changes is possible, and such an understanding is of course prone to rapid obsolescence. Nevertheless, a reading can – and should – be attempted. This book takes a intentionally subjective stance: it is structured around a series of conversations with architects and designers from China, South Korea and Japan. Especially in the case of China, as short a time as ten years ago many of these practices didn't exist, meaning the only environmental constant in their short lives has been change. A premise of this book is that a broad representation of uncertainty, related through personal experiences, can offer a more useful and compelling insight into a given context at a certain moment than an encyclopaedic yet impersonal compendium of factual documentation.

What these three countries don't have in common is just as fascinating as what they do. While the recent histories of all three are characterised by processes of rapid economic growth, sudden exposure to global cultural influence and a precipitous reconfiguration of their social structures, these processes have begun sequentially, staggered over a period of sixty years, and have been played out over increasingly compressed time frames, each outdoing the seemingly unsurpassable rates of growth and transformation of the previous one.

With regards to the countries not visited in this book, it is necessary to qualify the selection criteria. Together China, South Korea and Japan represent only a portion of the continent's architectural identity, albeit a meaningful one. But while India is the locus of transformations as rapid and globally significant as those occurring in China, and both Singapore and Taiwan are home to almost as many successful young architecture practices as Seoul, it is harder to carry out a clear reading of their societies or cultural identities through the collective body of work of the younger generation of architects. In many cases, there simply hasn't been the time for a mature architectural language to develop; in others, growth has perhaps not been conflictual enough to stimulate the desire for meaningful expression through design. Hong Kong's architects might be – in professional terms – more accomplished than China's, but for all their shortcomings the energy and creative vitality of China's designers makes them a far more fascinating and revealing subject.

It is impossible to speak of contemporary architecture in China without considering its relationship with the international media. The most visible expression of the country's uncontainable expansion is its architecture, and the media have seized upon it as a convenient and effective illustration for each episode in China's progressive creation of a new identity. In China architecture is demolished, rebuilt, criticised, confiscated, transformed, attacked and admired, always in the full view of the media. Be it a helicam shot of the oceans of high-rises germinating around the megalopolises of the Pearl River Delta, a rendered animation of the latest urban icon unveiled in front of a gasping audience by the celebrity architect of the moment, or a protest against the expropriation of vast swathes of residential Beijing, architecture is almost always an actor – and more often than not the protagonist – in the media's portrayal of contemporary China.

By the same token, members of an elite cadre of Chinese architects have achieved everything from increased international exposure to global stardom in part by virtue of the fact that they happen to be Chinese. In an essay published in *MAD Dinner*,[1] Jiang Jun (interviewed here on pp. 106–11) refers to what he defines as '"the Chineseness card", namely, the advantage of being a Chinese architect in an international architectural context'. This card plays into the hand of Chinese architects who, in the past decade, were savvy enough to realise that 'the world was gazing at China curiously, wondering what kind of "stars" would rise from the drastically changing Middle Kingdom, how their perspectives and manifestos would redefine China in a global context, and what kind of changes they would bring to the country'.

Jiang continues: 'One card that goes hand-in-hand with the Chineseness card is "the international card"', in other words a degree from a prestigious US or European university and work experience in top-ranking international design firms. This is perfectly compatible, he goes on to say, with 'China's strategy of importing/internalising foreign expertise so as to strengthen its presence on the world stage, known in the country as "bring-in-and-go-out"'. China is at present the largest market for architectural services in the world, and these young practices constitute a privileged category in this context. This 'fifth generation of Chinese architects ... [is] more relaxed about the identity issue; they regard both the West and China as their playground and combine both architectural styles in a more spontaneous manner', Linda Vlassenrood writes in her introductory essay to the catalogue of *China Contemporary*,[2] a recent exhibition at NAi Rotterdam.

Chinese architectural practices, in the contemporary understanding of the word, are a product of modernity, with the first generation of Chinese architects appearing after 1925. As Yung Ho Chang points out,[3] modernity is not a force from within – it is synonymous with a process of 'opening up' to outside influences, mainly from the West. Chang, who studied architecture in America, was himself instrumental in introducing to China a category of practice that today is relatively commonplace, but until a couple of decades ago was entirely non-existent: the small independent architecture office. When he founded Atelier Feichang Jianzhu ('unusual architecture' or 'amazing architecture') in 1993, it was China's first independent architectural firm, and acted as a model for an entire generation of practitioners across the country. It was this category of small practices (as opposed to the vast, State-owned design firms) that raised the question of what exactly constitutes 'Chineseness' in the context of modernity.

In the wake of decades of tentative experiments to hybridise new construction techniques and token emblems of 'Chineseness' (typically, a reinforced slab building topped by curved pitched roofs), these small independent practices upheld the notion that tradition was to be sought in the spatial disposition, proportions, design methodologies or materials rather than in the insertion of formal emblems. Young architects holding the previously mentioned 'international card' were anxious to express themselves through the vocabulary picked up in Western schools and offices: Princeton, Harvard, the Architectural Association, UCLA, the office of Zaha Hadid, OMA, Norman Foster and so on. Observing the work of these practices, the most interesting are the ones that relinquish all formal references to restrictive notions of 'tradition' and concentrate instead on creating contextual links in a conceptual sense, or by allowing the constraints and opportunities of available construction methodologies to influence the design. An exquisite example of this is Qingyun Ma's Father's House (see pp. 96–105): entirely devoid of token 'Chineseness', it is a beautiful and delicate essay on the potential of materials available on site, local unskilled labour and subtle references to the architecture of an era when there were no architects. In this situation, redesigning the process of communication with the construction workers through specially developed diagrams became just as critical to achieving a culturally relevant mode of expression as the use of overtly Chinese forms. In many cases, the limited amount of skilled labour available in China particularly in rural areas, combined with the inaccessibility of many of the latest building technologies, actually constitutes a stimulus towards innovation rather than a limitation or constraint.

Another force that architects in China must necessarily reckon with is the ubiquitous and pervasive sense of uncertainty that permeates every aspect of the country's identity, to the extent that it almost constitutes a subchapter of national policy. Today's China is the product of chaos, disorder and speed, but these apparent limitations are the symptoms of a phenomenal measure of energy. In his essay 'Learning from Uncertainty',[4] Chang sets out three steps for harnessing the creative potential of uncertainty, a gesture that in itself is profoundly Chinese in its pragmatism: '1. Learn to live with uncertainty; 2. Learn to take advantage of it; 3. Enjoy uncertainty'. Uncertainty is therefore perceived as an ungovernable contextual element, not dissimilar to the weather, to which value judgements cannot be usefully applied, and which has potentially positive connotations. Chang continues: 'The present-day Chinese situation is dynamic to the point of instability ... I have no time for either optimism or pessimism. I reflect, in order to move onto the next design challenge'.

The result might be schizophrenic and at times erratic, but it is also energetic, unrestrained and anti-dogmatic. In a situation in which geographic obstacles to demographic flow are gradually disappearing, this can be an advantage, as architects find themselves obliged to embrace a social context of permanent change. Today China's cities are the destination of the most extensive – and probably the most rapid – migrations of recent history, and the result is a condition of exacerbated contrast that has divided the country into two entities that coexist in close physical proximity. The disparities are so great as to suggest that speaking of China as a single entity is a misconception: on the one hand there is the countryside, poor in assets, infrastructure, technology and know-how; on the other there are the cities, which for all the inequalities they engender have become generators of wealth for a burgeoning middle class.

However schizophrenic, though, the vibrancy emanating from the Asian hotbed of urban experimentation is palpable, and the West is increasingly bewitched by it. An interesting upshot of this is the appearance of the intellectual protagonists of Asia's renaissance in the top positions of some of the best universities in the United States. In 2005, MIT's School of Architecture in Boston kicked off a trend by appointing Yung Ho Chang as Dean; this announcement was followed in rapid succession by Hitoshi Abe appearing at the helm of UCLA and Qingyun Ma at the lead of South California University's School of Architecture. More and more relatively recent Asian graduates from US and European universities are being lured back to their alma maters by professorships, or at the very least as participants in the international lecture circuit. As Jiang Jun points out, the 'Chineseness' card is particularly effective in attracting *a priori* fascination in an international audience: there is almost the sense that the West's slightly disorientated architectural circle, weary of its own stars and controversies and envious of China's youthful energy, wishes to distil and appropriate the elixir of its youthful vigour by installing Asia's most brilliant minds in positions of power, presumably in the hope that the raw energy will trickle down the ranks to its own new stock of designers.

The identity of the younger generation of Asian architects is inextricably connected to the precipitous social, political and cultural changes that have sequentially shaped and reshaped the continent, particularly China, in the last five decades. A short essay by Rem Koolhaas published in an exhibition catalogue of work by MADA s.p.a.m., the Shanghai-based practice founded by Qinyun Ma, describes some of the 'extreme [educational] experiences' Ma's generation was subjected to. In little more than a decade, Koolhaas points out, Ma's contemporaries experienced the closing of schools during the Cultural Revolution, the subsequent reinstatement of the schools and vindication of the intellectuals, and ultimately, for a select few, the opportunity to travel to America to enjoy a specialist Ivy League university training. Citing personal experience, Koolhaas argues that the intensity of this educational experience lends this generation intellectual temper and versatility:

'A special intelligence and a huge ingenuity are created by straddling apparent contradictions. [Ma's] is a generation that does not wait for rights to be formalised but simply assumes them. No generation in the history of the world has compressed so many contradictory experiences – or rather, learned so much from opposing worldviews – in such a short period. That is why they now carry Cyclopean burdens with such ease: the Beijing Olympics is the responsibility of a single woman, who criss-crosses the city on a scooter, armed with a laptop and an array of time, place, and audience-specific PowerPoint presentations. A colossal building is the responsibility of a former TV presenter who then studied international law…'.

One of the effects of this 'special intelligence' and remarkable versatility is that in many cases the notion of 'style' is precluded by an understanding of design as a strategy of arbitration between opposing or contradictory forces. For this reason the West's apparatus of architecture criticism at times finds itself at something of a loss when attempting to evaluate a contemporary practice's oeuvre. Any critic would be hard-pressed to find any kind of distinguishable stylistic continuity in the work of a large proportion of the architects in this book (especially Chinese), but to attempt to do so would be to miss a fundamental point: here both the architectural artefact and the conceptual drive that generates it are primarily defined not by aesthetic considerations but by an understanding of architecture as a form of 'built mediation' between the forces at play, and this mediation can have no predetermined outcome. For some, the avoidance of aesthetic 'habits' is incidental, almost accidental; for others, it is increasingly synonymous with a position of rebellion against the 'objectscape' of contemporary Asian cities, where signature architecture has been increasingly co-opted as a tool for urban branding. As the notorious pan-Asian urbanisation continues, somewhat alarmingly, to accelerate, architects are increasingly expected to make a choice. On the one hand, they can join the ranks of the high-output offices that regurgitate the repetitious, mundane and lucrative real estate that is the raw fodder of urban expansion; alternatively, they can bid to become the superstar authors of the iconic, media-friendly architectural antidotes to the anonymity of sprawl that events such as the Beijing Olympics of 2008 occasion.

The work of many of these younger architects and smaller practices stands in stark contrast to this perceived dichotomy. For example, Atelier Bow-Wow's writings on the densification of Tokyo's urban core offer an excellent synopsis of the conundrums confronting cities across Asia at all stages of development. As a result of a population shift back to the urban centres following a dispersal into the suburbs, developer-built skyscrapers are springing up in ever-increasing numbers around the extremely central but traditionally village-like districts of Marunouchi, Shiodome, Shinagawa and Roppongi. This construction frenzy is encouraged by the falling land prices and reduced building costs resulting from the prolonged recession, not to mention the neo-liberalist, developer-friendly stance of the government with regards to urban planning exemplified by the 'Law on Special Measures for Urban Renaissance' passed in 2002. While densification of a city's urban core might in other circumstances be considered a positive trend, Yoshiharu Tsukamoto argues that in this case it marks the end of a characteristically Japanese resistance to planning and small-scale intervention that had come to define Tokyo's urban fabric since the end of WW2. The Metabolist movement, he points out, was the last modernist attempt to transform the city, and its effects can be described as tangible only on an infrastructural scale. The vast majority of Tokyo's small-scale residential and commercial buildings, on the other hand, are the result of a semi-spontaneous process of contextual negotiation.

The danger posed by the developer-driven construction boom, Tsukamoto argues, is that it inevitably entails a shift in scale that precludes the presence of non-corporate entities such as the family-run stores or the small-scale enterprise, which in turn tends to delimit the active use of public space and the affinity of local communities. Policy, more than anything else, will dictate the destiny of these neighbourhoods, but there are times when even architects who are not on the payroll of developers find themselves actively implicated in the debate, particularly when it comes to making choices regarding permanence versus impermanence. As is well known, the short life span of its buildings constitutes one of Japan's architectural idiosyncrasies, and to this day the 'scrap and build' policy (i.e. the frequent demolishing and reconstruction of buildings, particularly dwellings) remains the norm. Tokyo's urban fabric is perpetually regenerated, fragment by fragment and day by day, in a process not dissimilar to the way skin cells die and are replaced. Despite the numerous critics of this practice, Tsukamoto and one of his graduate students, Jorge Almazán, argue that – beyond the obvious benefits of its inherent adaptability – it is the one reason the Japanese capital's urban fabric has resisted corporatisation for so long. 'Like the big Western capitals, London or Paris, Rome or New York, [Tokyo's] new mega-redevelopments are made as stable monumental objects to last centuries. They are conceived in an effort to overcome the common Tokyo mentality of "scrap and build", the name given to the phenomenon of often replacing buildings with new ones, in a city where buildings of 25 years are considered old. ... Much of the quality, character and dynamism of this city are based on the continuous renovation of its building stock. ... The soft urban structure of Tokyo, based on the "scrap and build" practice and its mixed residential areas, generates an energy not found in the European and American cities, creating a living environment, spatial structure and lifestyle with a unique character.'[5] Embracing it is emblematic, in their eyes, of the particular openness of some architects towards the unique complexity and fragility of a city that is neither hostile nor chaotic; a position that stands in contrast to the 'defensive attitude of certain Japanese architects, represented by Tadao Ando and his bare concrete houses'. As for the value of historical preservation, they ask, isn't 'scrap and build' in itself a traditional Japanese practice to be itself preserved?

Despite having both been practically razed to the ground in not-too-distant timeframes, the Japanese and South Korean capitals developed according to radically different patterns during the last five or six decades, and small-scale, short-life-span architecture never became a feature of Seoul. It would be impossible to comprehend the contemporary architectural culture of South Korea, and the ideas expressed by many of the Korean architects interviewed in this book, without bearing in mind the entity of the transformations the nation underwent in the course of the second half of the twentieth century. Long known as the 'hermit kingdom', Korea had virtually no contact with Western culture until its ports were opened under external military pressure in 1876. For the first half of the twentieth century, the policies of the Japanese occupiers gave rise to the perception of Modernism as a cultural instrument being introduced with the objective of supplanting Korean culture. The end of the occupation, which coincided with the end of WW2, was followed in relatively short order by the crippling destruction of the Korean War, a three-year conflict that left the nation divided, bankrupt and deprived of virtually every kind of infrastructure.

Fast forward to 2008, and the magnitude of the transformation witnessed by Korean society becomes apparent. South Korea's economy is the third largest in Asia and the eleventh largest in the world. In what is referred to as the 'Miracle on the Han River', the nation's GDP per capita grew from only $100 in 1963 to $10,000 in 1995, surging on to $25,000 in 2007. A key turning point in this narrative is the success of the 1986 Asian Games and the 1988 Olympic Games: vast amounts of capital injected into the nation's infrastructure gave many architects, largely under the aegis of the atelier-style architectural cooperative Space Group, their first major opportunity to exhibit large-scale works on an international stage.

Seoul's particular brand of urban expansion might no longer command the overexposure China has become accustomed to, but that's not to say that it is less staggering. Over the past fifty years, 80% of the population has relocated to the cities – well beyond the global average of 50%. It is a nation of contradictions and overlapping identities: Shamanism, Catholicism and Confucianism all exert powerful influences on society, blending elements of pop culture, religion, philosophy and superstition into a singularly multifaceted worldview. Since the mid- to late 1990s, this and many other aspects of Korean culture became familiar to the vast majority of other Asian nations thanks to the 'Korean Wave' phenomenon that transformed the country into the continent's largest exporter of media and entertainment. Quasi-miraculous economic growth, however, has come at a cost: it is a ruthlessly competitive and quantity-driven society, taken by the market economy to the point of obsession. As Minsuk Cho points out (see pp. 115–22), uncompromising segregation based on material wealth coupled with exorbitant real-estate prices manifests itself in disquieting architectural artefacts such as vertical gated communities and indistinguishable batteries of Hilberseimer-like tower blocks. Perhaps as a reaction to this, much of Korea's contemporary architecture is light, at times even jocular, appearing almost to be more in tune with the anime movies the country exports to the surrounding region than with the urban fabric of its capital, Seoul.

Each of the buildings and stories presented in this book is a point of departure rather than a point of arrival, a place from which to observe Asia's cities, buildings and people. We sought to avoid too superficial a reading: it is tempting but misguided to try to understand or even measure change using the yardstick of formal innovation. This is not to say that innovation is not to be found, and in certain instances it may be even formal, but a search for an aesthetic of 'Asian-ness' was certainly not the objective of this project. For this reason the photographic language used to represent the selected architecture is, to some extent, unconventional for a book of this kind: it avoids the heroic and spectacular depictions preferred by editorial convention (and, only too often, by architects themselves) in favour of a subtler and more intimate expression. Images are unavoidably incapable of spanning the vast gap between the reader and the physical reality of the building, but by representing them 'as found', and not in the perfection of their inaugural condition, we hope to bring them one small but significant measure closer.

[1] Brendan McGetrick and Chen Shu Yu (eds.), *MAD Dinner* (Barcelona: ACTAR, 2006).

[2] Christine de Baan, Huang Du, Jaap Guldemond, Garrie van Pinxteren and Linda Vlassenrood (eds.), *China Contemporary: Architecture, Art, Visual Culture* (Rotterdam: NAi Publishers, 2006).

[3] Preface to Ian Luna and Thomas Tsang, *On the Edge: Ten Architects from China* (New York: Rizzoli, 2006).

[4] *Area*, special issue on China.

[5] *Scrap and Build: Alternatives to the Corporate Redevelopment of Tokyo*, Harvard publication.

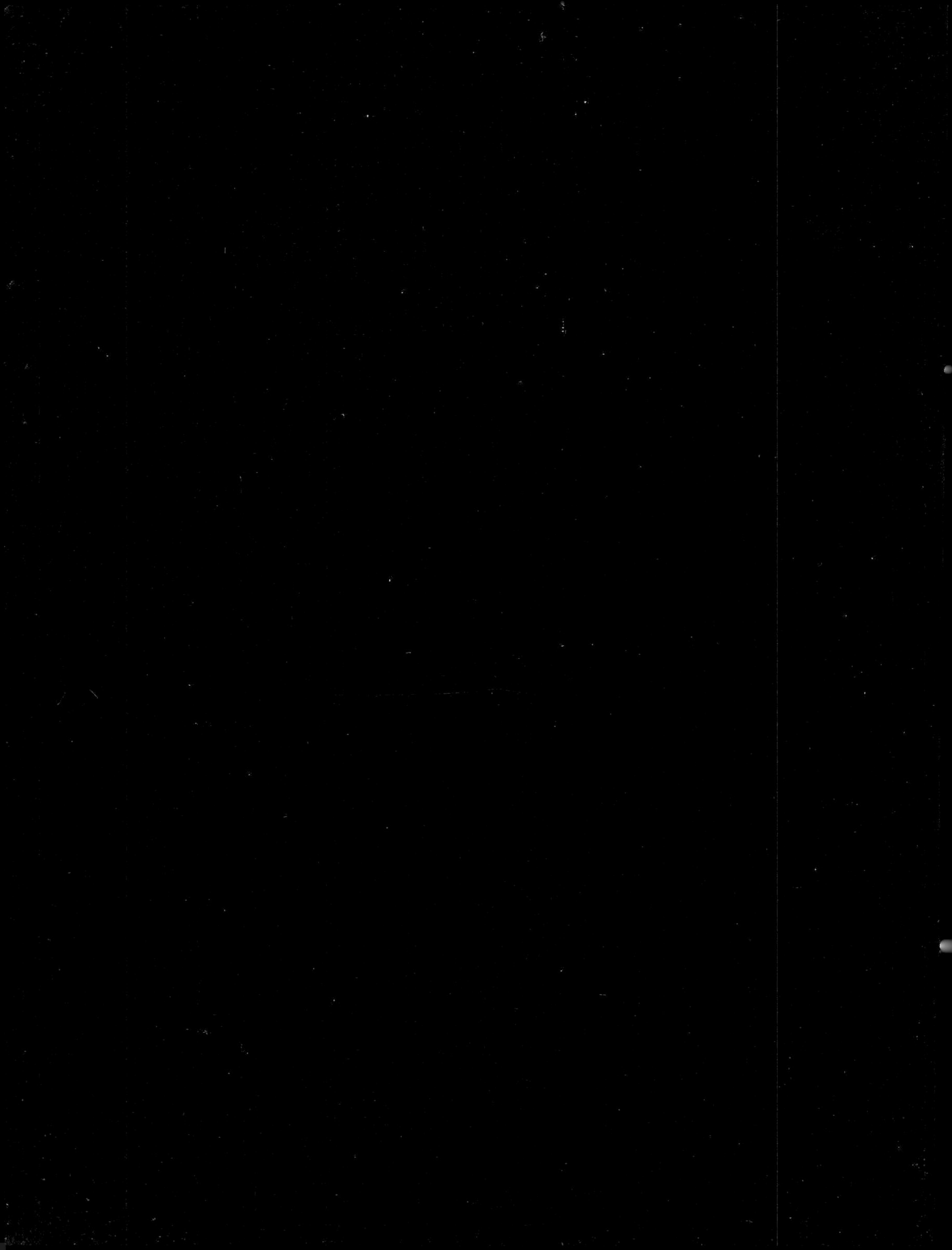

CHINA

Qun Dang

Qun Dang (MAD Design, Beijing)

MAD is one of the most international young practices operating from China today. Could you tell us how the office was born?

MAD Design has three partners – Yansong Ma, Yosuke Hayano and myself. Ma was the founding partner. He registered the practice in the United States a long time ago under the name Ma Design, and then changed the name to MAD when Yosuke Hayano and I joined. One thing we have in common is that we all studied at foreign universities. Ma and I got our graduate degrees in the US, and Yosuke graduated from the AA in London. Yosuke and Ma met each other while working for Zaha Hadid. They worked there together for a year, and then moved back to China. MAD officially opened on 1 April 2004, which makes the office almost four years old now.

The first two years were very difficult, mostly because the kind of design work we do is totally unfamiliar in China. It was very hard to get commissions. We did a lot of competitions to keep ourselves busy, which ultimately resulted in us winning the competition for the Absolute Towers in Toronto. That was a real breakthrough for the office. The Absolute Towers got so much international press that we're actually getting more commissions than we can handle. This is quite ironic, because although we have several projects that are nearing construction stage, the only finished one is a clubhouse just outside Beijing. This wouldn't be too unusual in any other country, but for an architecture practice to have completed only one small building in three years is unheard of in China. Most practices would have built millions of square feet by now.

Was it a deliberate strategy to build so little?

Yes. Building in China involves a number of complications, so we're very selective about the projects we take on. It's something we've discussed a lot with other architects – you design something, and when you finally manage to build it, the owner or developer changes everything. It's the same all over China, and it's very frustrating. I guess it'll change someday. In the meantime, the situation for architects isn't at all easy. It's not just a matter of luck, either. If all you're interested in is square feet, you can get a lot built in a short time. But if you insist on a certain level of design quality, it's probably harder to achieve than in any other country.

That's paradoxical, if you think about it. Many Western architects complain about the constraints imposed by strict building codes, and yearn for the looser codes you have here in China.

This is just one of the many paradoxes involved with working in China. Another is the issue of preservation. Outside the first or second ring road in Beijing, you can build pretty much whatever you like. Inside, you can't touch anything because it's now considered a historical district. This leads to unbelievable contrasts between the buildings used by tourists or wealthy outsiders, that are pristine, and the areas inhabited by locals, that don't even have showers or toilets. Many neighbourhoods are frozen in a permanent condition of squalor as an effect of 'preservation'. It's an issue we are investigating at the moment through a research project entitled *Beijing 2050*.

Tell us about Hong Luo Clubhouse, the project you mentioned you have recently completed.

The clubhouse sits in a small lake on the outskirts of Beijing, and its main purpose is to serve as a meeting place for the club's members. The building is like an island with two branches – one is a swimming pool floating on the lake, the other is an accessible platform that sits below water level. The architectural form is determined by the circulation pattern: two major routes converge at the centre of the clubhouse and reach all the way up along an ascending roof. The flat surface of the lake melts into the curve of the roof, expressing the transition from liquid to solid. The shape of the roof is a projection of the linear, functional organisation of the ground level's programme, and the main access to the clubhouse leads visitors along a path set 1.3 metres below water level, giving them the impression they are walking in the lake. The outdoor swimming pool is also submerged into the lake, so as to keep the two water levels even. The most difficult thing about this project was finding a contractor who would take it on. Most refused, simply because they didn't know how to build it.

Hong Luo Clubhouse
Architects: MAD (Yansong Ma, Yosuke Hayano, Qun Dang)
Location: Beijing
Client: Beijing Earth Real Estate Develops Company
Programme: private clubhouse
Building area: 487.2 sqm
Design team: Shen Jun, Christian Taubert,
Marco Zuttioni, Yu Kui

Do you think the 2008 Olympics in Beijing will be a turning point for contemporary architecture in China?

Yes, of course. The new CCTV headquarters and Herzog & de Meuron's stadium are high-quality projects that demonstrate that world-class designs can be executed here, and ultimately this will help young practices like ours by raising the awareness of the value of design. But in any case we see MAD as an international more than a Chinese practice. We intend to open a branch office in Tokyo soon, and we have projects under way in several countries outside Asia. And we exhibit a lot: we had our first solo show last year at the Venice Architecture Biennale, and we'll be opening another solo exhibition in Denmark shortly, hosted by the Association of Danish Architects.

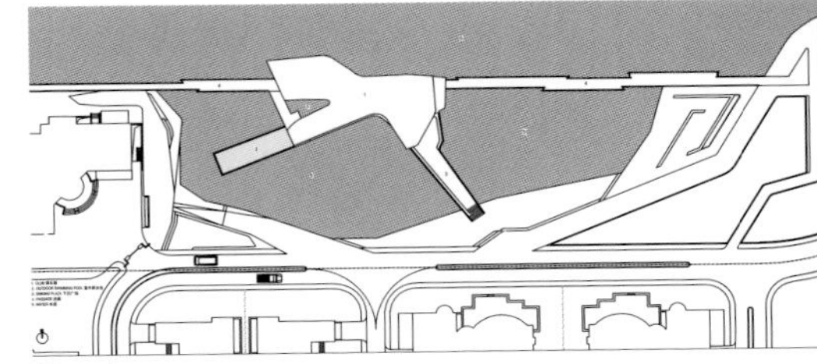
Site plan

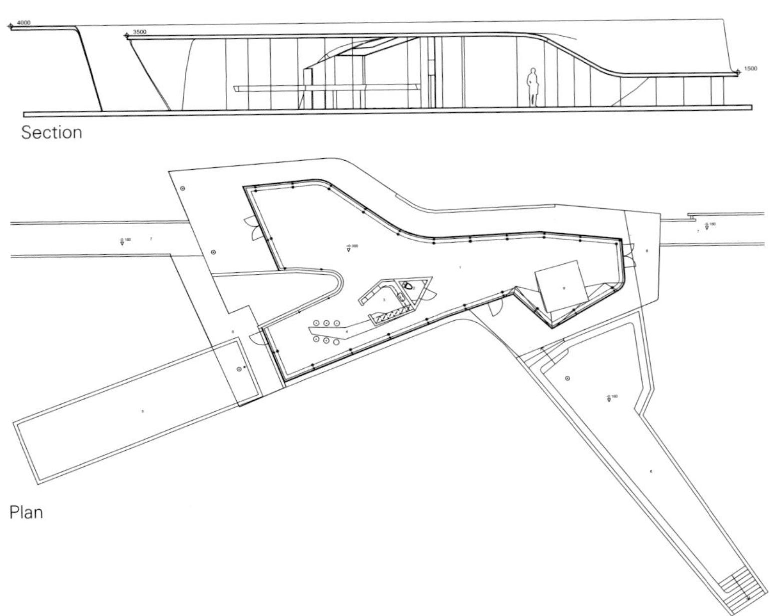

Section

Plan

The floor of Hong Luo Clubhouse, in the suburbs of Beijing, is sunk 1,300 mm below the surface of Hong Luo Lake. The building also comprises a small swimming pool that floats within the lake (see p. 29)

Liu Jiakun

Liu Jiakun (Beijing)

One of your most remarkable projects is the Luyeyuan Stone Sculpture Art Museum in the Sichuan province. One could almost say it is a sculpture in itself.

The museum houses a collection of stone sculptures, so the architecture is an attempt to evoke the idea of 'artificial stone'. That was certainly one of the reasons I chose raw concrete. The museum's galleries are designed around a central atrium, and subtle relationships are created between natural daylight, the landscape and the exhibits themselves by carefully modulating the gaps between the blocks that constitute the building. The site of this building, a field between a river and the woods, is composed of four areas. The museum is on the largest of the four, and the other three are used for parking, open-air exhibitions and services. Bamboo divides each zone from the others, giving a sense of intimacy. A series of winding paths lead visitors around the museum and through the bamboo, ending at the main entrance above the lotus pond.

What were the other reasons for choosing raw concrete as the base material?

As skilled labour is quite scarce in this part of China, I decided to build a frame structure and use naked concrete and shale bricks for the vertical surfaces. Because of the rough construction technology, it's very hard to ensure the perpendicularity of the walls when pouring the concrete. But if you build the interior brick walls first, they can serve as a formwork when pouring the outer concrete walls, and in this way the perpendicularity is ensured. Very rough wood was used for the formwork so to create the distinctive striation on the vertical concrete surfaces. This dense, irregular pattern also serves to hide defects in the pouring technique. What I was looking for was a meeting point between contemporary architectural aesthetics and the building technology available locally. One has to take into consideration the realities facing architects building in China today.

Another thing is that it isn't unusual here for buildings to undergo frequent alterations as the programmatic requirements change over time. Masterplans are often poorly conceived, and buildings either have to adapt or face demolishing. Many of the interior surfaces are built using a mixture of bricklaying and plastering techniques, and this makes them much more adaptable to change than a raw concrete surface.

What is your relationship with other architects of your generation?

I decided to study architecture without really knowing what architecture was or what architects actually did, and I was only remotely interested in buildings. I was much more fascinated by the literary world, and over the years I published several novels. When I finally decided to practise architecture, about ten years ago, I found I had a broader, more diversified view of society than many other designers. I also had another system to compare architecture to, the world of literature, and this was an invaluable source of inspiration for me. Even today, most of my friends are writers.

What changes have you seen in China in these ten years?

This is a unique period in Chinese history, and I doubt there will ever be another like it. Architecture as a discipline has been reborn in China in the past ten years – prior to that it almost didn't exist for many decades. Until ten years ago, I could never have been attracted by design, but right now I see it as the most powerful expression of the incredible energy and complexity that characterises Chinese society today.

The climate in Chengdu, where the Luyeyuan Stone Sculpture Art Museum is located, is semi-tropical. To reach the entrance visitors must follow a path through the woods and cross a narrow bridge, which then continues through the building (see p. 34)

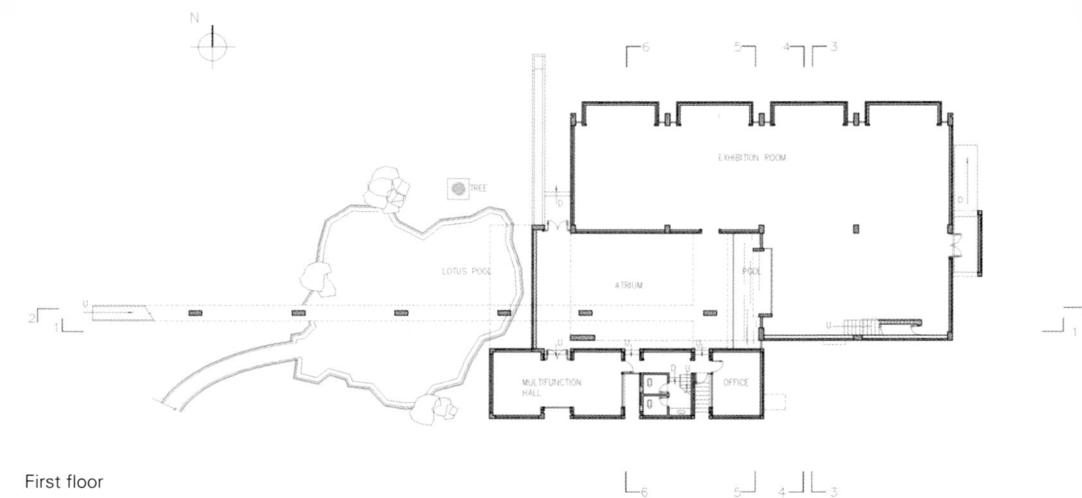

First floor

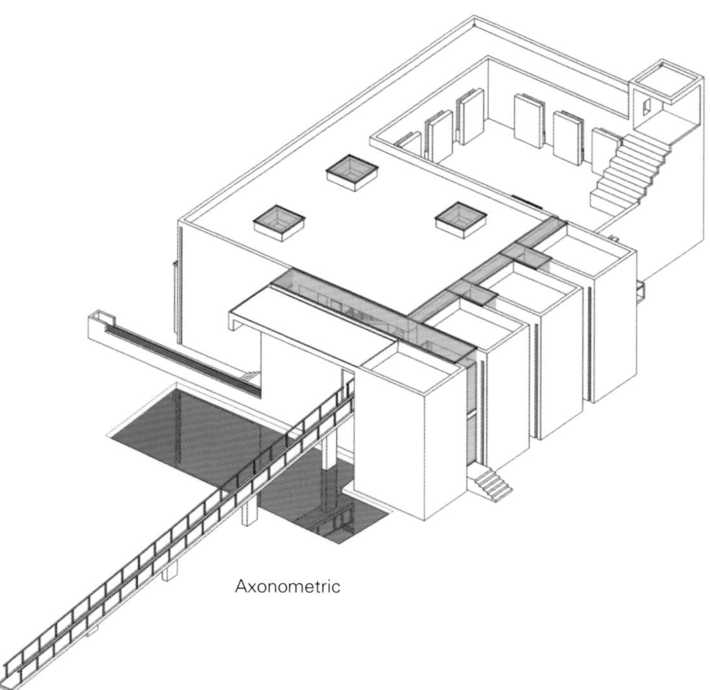

Axonometric

Luyeyuan Stone Sculpture Art Museum
Architects: Liu Jiakun (with Wang Lun)
Location: Yunqiao village, Xinmin town, Pi county, Chengdu, Sichuan
Site area: 6,670 sqm
Building area: 1,037 sqm
Floor area (main building): 990 sqm
Client: Zhong Ming
Contractor: GoArchit Art Engineering Co. Ltd, Sichuan
Structure: reinforced concrete, shale brick, pebble, blue stone, glass, steel

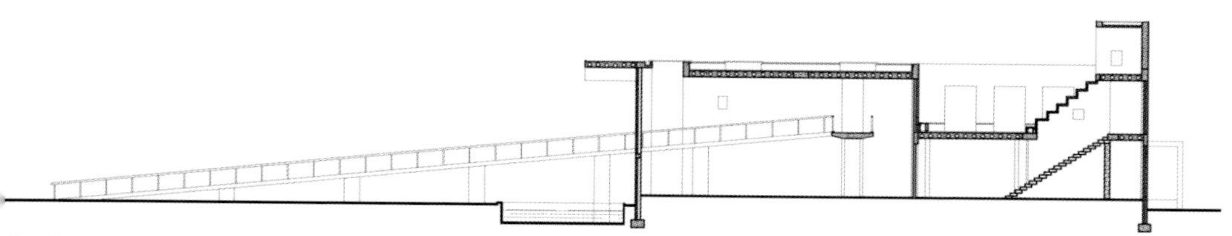

Section 1–1

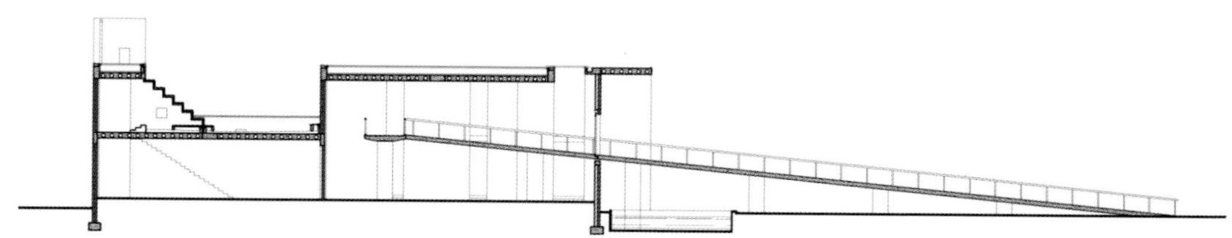

Section 2–2

Jianchuan Museum Aggregation, Anren, Sichuan

Zhang Ke

Zhang Ke (standardarchitecture, Beijing)

standardarchitecture, founded in 1999, is a professional partnership formed by a group of young designers from China and Europe with an interest in architecture, landscape architecture, interior and industrial design. Originally established in New York, the firm has gradually relocated its main base to Beijing, after receiving several large commissions there.

Your largest completed project to date, Wuhan CR-land French–Chinese Art Centre, is the result of an unusual brief. Can you tell us about it?

It's actually quite an amusing story. The building started out its existence as a temporary salesroom for a nearby high-rise apartment complex. It was the year of French–Chinese cultural exchange, and shortly after it was completed I was giving a presentation to the French consul on a cruise boat on the Yangtze River, and he fell in love with the building. He was very keen to find a way to keep it. I convinced the developer to donate it to the government, and the government then agreed to lend it to the French consulate. It now houses two exhibition spaces, one in the east and one in the west hall.

The site of the art centre is directly opposite the Wuchang Tanhualin area, not far from the Yangtze River. It's a very inspiring place: Wuhan was traditionally home to many of China's greatest intellectuals, and many of them lived in this neighbourhood. This is where the Chinese industrial revolution began, and where the Chinese Communist Party and the Red Army were formed. For a long time Wuhan was one of the richest trade centres in China, which also explains why there are so many French companies buildings here.

The expectation was for the building to become an important public gathering point for the city and a monument to its ongoing transformation.

We were interested in testing the possibilities of designing something using ink-washing, one of the techniques employed by the Chinese intellectuals who used to reside in the area. So we did a very loose ink-wash drawing that we later scanned and literally transposed onto the façade of the building as a pattern of slits.

Why did you choose the bridge configuration?

When we started to consult with the local planning bureau they told us there was a thirty-metre-wide storm trench on the site that couldn't be enclosed but could be built over. This gave us the idea of using the trench as a kind of water-garden that would dissect the site, and then floating a long enclosed bridge over it to connect the east and west halls. Because of the length of the bridge's span and the building's unusual slitted skin, there were considerable challenges in deciding how to arrange the steel structural members inside the concrete. The chief engineer told us it would take a computer six months to calculate how to optimally arrange the steel members, so we had to find another solution. We invited some engineering PhD students from the local university to take up the challenge. They solved the problem empirically using a scale model, and we successfully achieved a 32-metre span at the centre. Just after the construction work was completed Wuhan was struck by an earthquake, but the building was unscathed.

Like many others of your generation, you studied and practised abroad before returning to China to set up a practice. What kind of relationship exists between architects of your age, with an international outlook, and those of the previous generation? How has architectural culture changed in China over the past fifty years?

In general we are no longer so naïve as to believe that architecture can single-handedly change society. It's rarely discussed, but it's a burden and responsibility generations prior to ours had to deal with. A big problem with the slightly older generation of architects is that they sold visionary concepts without genuinely considering the utility of realising them. I think it's fundamental that we recognise the limitations and potentials of our profession: I don't honestly think we are the driving force of society, but we do have our responsibilities. What we can do is change the physical environment and improve the landscape and the cities we inhabit, and this is already a lot. We are trying to emphasise the importance of actually building a new reality, and this is clearly in contrast with the older generation. Independent practices are designing a tiny fraction of the architecture that's being built in China. The huge design institutes that were, and largely still are, State-owned are still carrying out the bulk of the design work. There are a lot of clichés about being an architect here today. We're no longer interested in topics that were relevant to older generations. We're no longer interested in imitating stylistic traits of the big names of Western architecture. We're not even interested in mimicking the way they run their offices. We don't care about trying to distinguish or differentiate

Western and Chinese architecture. We don't even care about thinking in terms of generations. The idea of making something really Chinese for the sole purpose of exhibiting in the West doesn't interest us… In this sense, 'Chineseness' really doesn't matter to us. We care more about introducing innovation into the actual building process. We might, at certain points, establish a dialogue with tradition and explore new ways of using traditional materials, but it's not a precondition.

What do you think about the widespread destruction of traditional buildings and Communist-era architecture that is going on around you? In your opinion, will the architectural memory of this era eventually be lost forever?

Watching all the *hutongs* and courtyard buildings disappear from this city made me very critical of the demolition process for a while. But now I'm not. At this point I'm actually optimistic, because as soon as the continuity of the old urban fabric disappears, that kind of urbanism becomes pointless. Keeping those areas would simply create preservationist enclaves. That city is already gone, it's already totally fragmented, and a new framework is already in place. Yes, it survives in the memory of a small group of people, but in reality it's already gone. There is another danger now that could be even worse than demolition of the historical districts – we call it 'popular originalism'. It calls for the preservation of a few 'historical' districts, but encourages the demolition of recent architecture. Whatever happened in history, there is a reason why it happened, and a lot of that is being removed. There is a reason why we should remember it – even Communist history, even ugliness: it's still history, and selectively erasing history is almost worse than erasing it entirely. This policy is spreading like a virus. Right now is possibly the worst moment for this part of China, but I don't think it will get any worse. You could describe this era as the Urban Revolution, as opposed to the Cultural Revolution – it's happening all over China, and the fact that it looks so chaotic is part of the process of reorganisation.

Zhang Hong

Watercolour sketch of the façade

Plan

Wuhan CRland French–Chinese Art Centre
Architects: standardarchitecture
Location: Wuchang
Programme: exhibition space
Site area: 4,000 sqm
Building area: 1,500 sqm
Structure: reinforced concrete

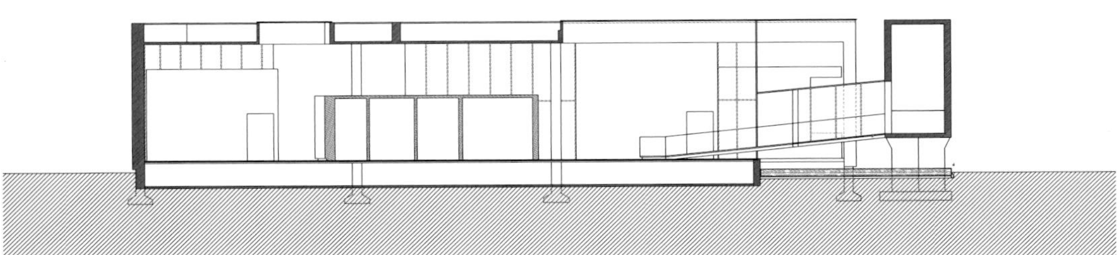

Section

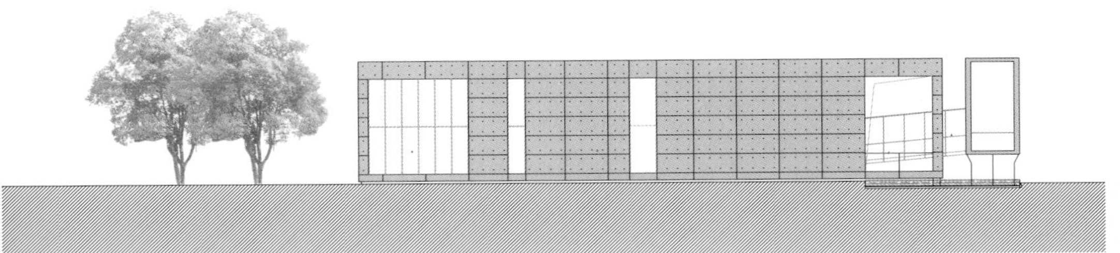

Section

Xiayu Kindergarten, Qingpu

Zhuang Shen and Liu Yichuin (Atelier Deshaus, Shanghai)

One of your most recent projects is the Xiayu Kindergarten in the Qingpu region. It's quite unusual both in size and layout. Can you say something about your design strategy?

The kindergarten contains fifteen classes, which we treated as the building blocks for the scheme. Each unit has its own living room, dining room, bedroom and outdoor playground. In the design of the class units, we arranged all the living rooms and outdoor playgrounds on the ground floor and added brightly coloured boxes on the upper floor. These boxes serve as bedrooms for the children to rest in the afternoon. After placing all these functions in a row on this narrow site, we decided that a soft curve would suit the programme better than a straight line. We separated the fifteen classrooms and the staff's offices into two elongated clusters that embrace each other. A painted wall identifies the classrooms, while offices and special-purpose classrooms are enclosed by translucent glass panels. Finally, we wrapped the entire kindergarten with a wall to create a barrier against the noise coming from the nearby highway. To emphasise the impression that the coloured boxes float above the kindergarten, we detached them slightly from the roof of the first floor and scattered them over the length of the building. It was very important to us to introduce an element of uncertainty and randomness into the design, to make it human in some way. For the same reason, we linked the bedrooms in groups of three with raised wooden walkways. It helps create a friendly and human atmosphere – a bit like a village of bedrooms.

From an ideological point of view, what drives your practice? China seems to be one giant construction site, but very little good architecture is actually being built. How do you engage this situation?

Social ideals spurred the development of the Modernist revolution, and to bring true vigour and soul into today's architecture it seems clear that we have to seek out another ideal land. Maybe something to do with the preservation of our cultural identity. We're fascinated by the intersections and overlaps between contemporary architectural influences coming from the West and the unique tradition inherited from our history. It makes it necessary for us to remain aware of the changes occurring everyday around the world, and to understand and evaluate them as quickly as possible.

How?

By asking: What on earth fascinates us? What on earth still moves us? We realise that most of the knowledge in this field is imported from outside, yet our design must be native-born since we operate in a very particular context. I don't mean that we should become conservative – we should aim at transcending our native designs. Whatever your starting point, whatever your method, in the final analysis architecture is realised by spaces, volumes and surfaces, and therefore comes back to an issue of materiality. That's where other influences, local influences, come into play. Architectural design strives to evolve a totality out of numerous parts and details of different materials and functions. A detail might be impressive, but it is never as important as the totality of the building.

What is the normal relationship between what the client is after and the brief you are given and the way you can respond the project?

Normally we're contacted by a client – we haven't done many competitions. They often give us only a very basic set of programmatic requirements, so we end up creating the brief together. A lot of developers have money but have no idea how to develop or use the areas they own; that's why even before we start designing we advise them on how to best develop them.

Is it normal for this relationship to exist between architect and developer?

This happens quite often. The problem is that this kind of situation generates huge uncertainty... *Domus China* recently published a very good article by Yung Ho Chang on this subject. The developer buys the land, and at that point the government tells him how many cubic metres can be built on it. At the beginning of a project, we often have no idea *what* to design – only *how much* we are allowed to design. This situation is very specific to China. We're forced to consider how to design buildings to fit into rapidly changing environments. So the way we are designing is different from the past. It's very frustrating, but on the other hand it's also interesting...

Do you think the success of architects in China depends on whether they can design good architecture even without a programme?

It's an issue Chinese architects are facing now. Architects assume they will be given a brief and will design the building to suit a given function. When you don't have a brief, you are forced to conceive buildings that can adapt to an unstable, unpredictable environment. It can be a very interesting way to work. It boils down to the fact that function is no longer dictating form – how could it? If the function is always changing, what is the form? The building is the result of the interaction between three forces – architect, developer and government, often pulling in different directions.

Do you think this space of uncertainty in architecture opens up a certain creativity or potential?

It means that all your ideas are forced to continually adapt, which can be a good thing. The only certainty is that there's no sign of this situation changing.

Following pages
Located on the edge of Qingpu New Town, Xiayu Kindergarten is comprised of fifteen classrooms, each with its own living room, dining room, bedrooms and outdoor playgrounds. These clusters are scattered along an elongated plot located beside a river. The classrooms are on the ground floor, and the brightly coloured bedroom boxes are on the first floor.

pp. 58–59
Walkways connect the bedrooms above the roof of the classrooms

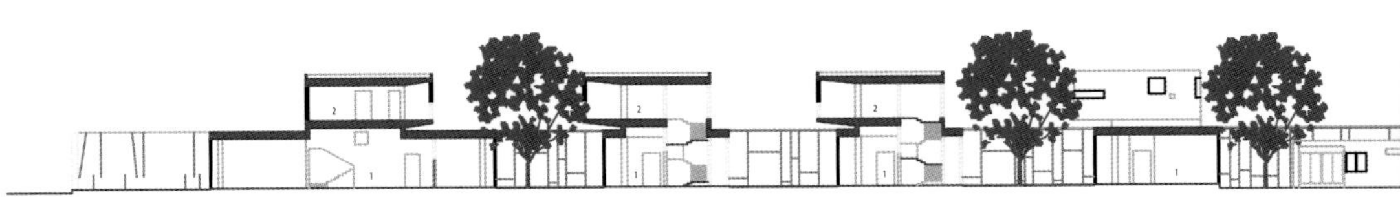

Longitudinal section

Xiayu Kindergarten
Architects: Atelier Deshaus
Location: Qingpu New Town, Shanghai
Design phase: 2003–4
Completed: November 2004
Floor area: 6,328 sqm

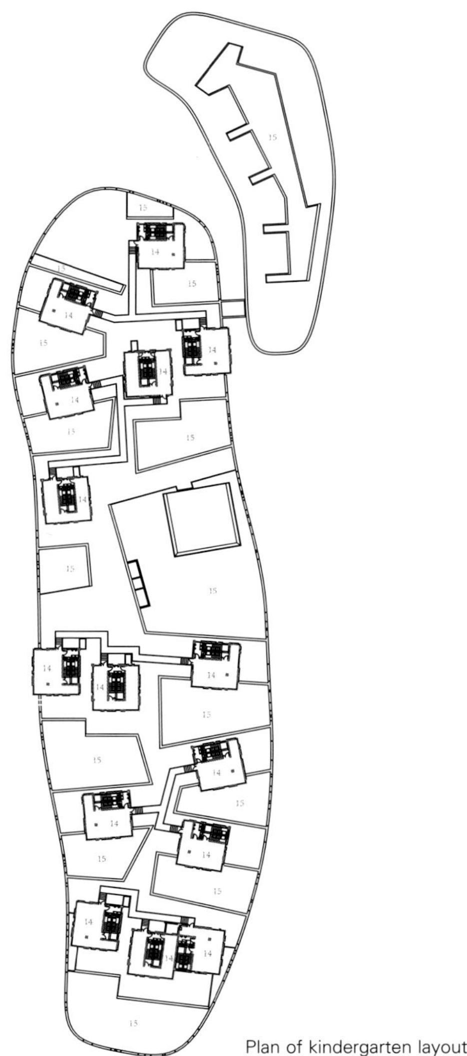

Plan of kindergarten layout

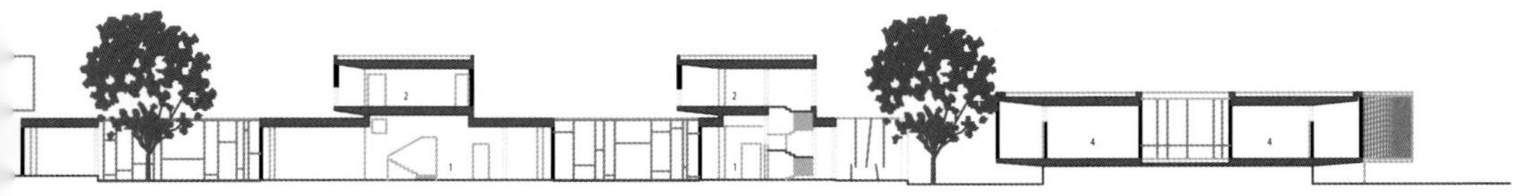

Xu Tiantian

Xu Tiantian (DnA Architects, Beijing)

In 1997, Xu Tiantian had just completed her Bachelor of Architecture at Tsinghua University in Beijing. Hoping to gain an international perspective on design practice, she moved to the States and signed up to the Masters Program at Harvard University Graduate School of Design. After a year working in a medium-size practice run by one of her professors in Boston, Xu moved on to Rotterdam, where she spent another year working at OMA.

What drove you to pack your bags and return to Asia? I guess you were hoping for a part of the action in China.

It actually happened when I decided to take a week's holiday in China back in 2003. The country was just recovering from SARS, and the energy in the air was real, was tangible. It was very different from when I left – there was excitement and enthusiasm everywhere. It was like a drug, something I'd never felt in the US or Holland. So I decided to come back, pretty much on the spot.

What was it like, returning to a country that had changed so much in such a short time? Did you set up your practice immediately?

It took time for me to adapt to the situation and the energy here. I didn't jump straight into my own practice – my early work was mainly in collaboration with Ai Weiwei on the Jinhua Sculpture Park. When I did decide to set up an independent practice, innumerable commercial projects were commissioned and then cancelled. It was very dispiriting.

Then one day I was approached by the director of an arts centre here in Beijing to design a new, contemporary version of the artists' villages that cropped up in Beijing in the last decade or two. It was to be an arts centre, a gallery and artists' studios, all in one, totalling 5,000 square metres. It was such a large project that I never expected it to actually be built. But it was, and it was fast-tracked as well – the whole project lasted less than a year, including design and construction.

Do you see this remarkable speed as a challenge or an opportunity?

Our initial proposal was submitted in two weeks, and the client signed off on it on the spot. He then told us he wanted to start excavating two weeks later. The intention behind the design was to bring together under a single roof the work of local Beijing artists, Chinese artists from other cities and international shows. The idea was to keep the traditional exhibition box format, but to scatter them across the site and connect them in various ways. The ground floor is quite enclosed but the upper floors have a lot of views and sky lights. The speed in China can be intimidating... The construction frenzy here is certainly an opportunity, but the problem is that you never know which of the hundreds of projects you design in two weeks will actually be realised. Apart from this, the greatest limitation to anyone working in China at the moment is the rudimentary building technology. There's no comparison with what you can achieve in Europe or the US.

What other projects are you working on at the moment?

I'm very excited about a project called Jiangyuan Shuian Villa. It's a private residence located on a vast Mongolian plane, on a site facing Kaokao Shina Lake in Erdos, Inner Mongolia. The given programme is very simple: the total building area is to be 1,200–1,500 square metres, and there will be five private suites, one for the owner and the others for guests. The site affects the project a lot – it's very different from urban China, very raw, very beautiful.

What do you think about being back in China?

I feel very lucky to be able to embrace the future, to embrace change, to embrace the incredible potential that there is in this place right now. You can feel the energy and the opportunities, but you have to put up with a lot of 'two-week projects' – commissions, some of them very large, that fall through after they've been in the office for less than a month. Also, anyone who has worked in the West becomes highly aware of the limitations of the local building and construction technologies. But that's the nature of the architectural profession – you have to work within the constraints.

SONGZHUANG ART CENTER

美術館

Songzhuang Art Center
Architects: DnA, Beijing
Location: Songzhuang, Beijing
Client: Xiaopu Village
Project team: Xu Tiantian, Yingnan Chen, Albert Chu
Building area: 5,000 sqm
Structure: reinforced concrete
Surface: brick

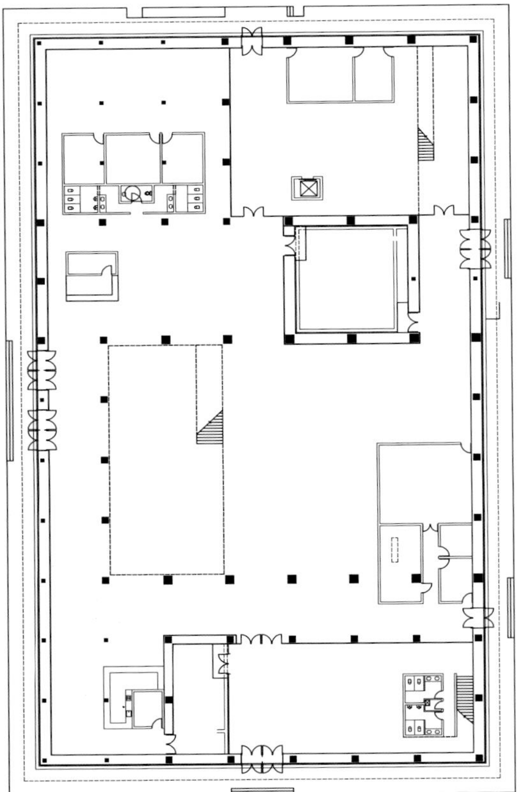

First floor plan

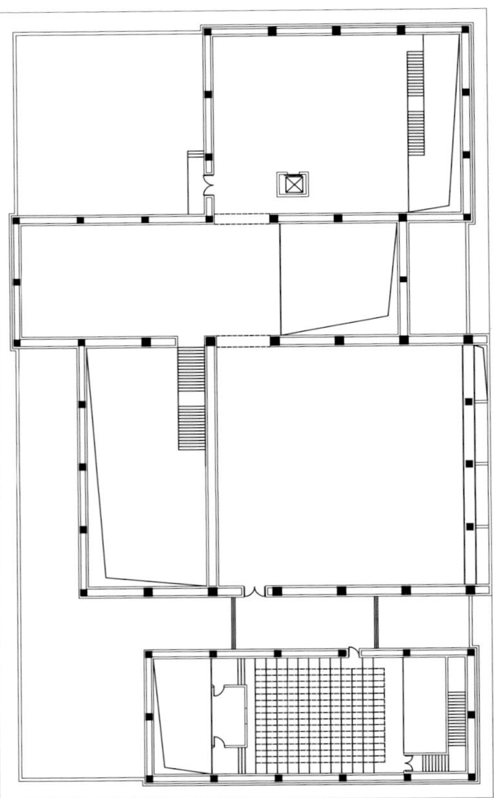

Second floor plan

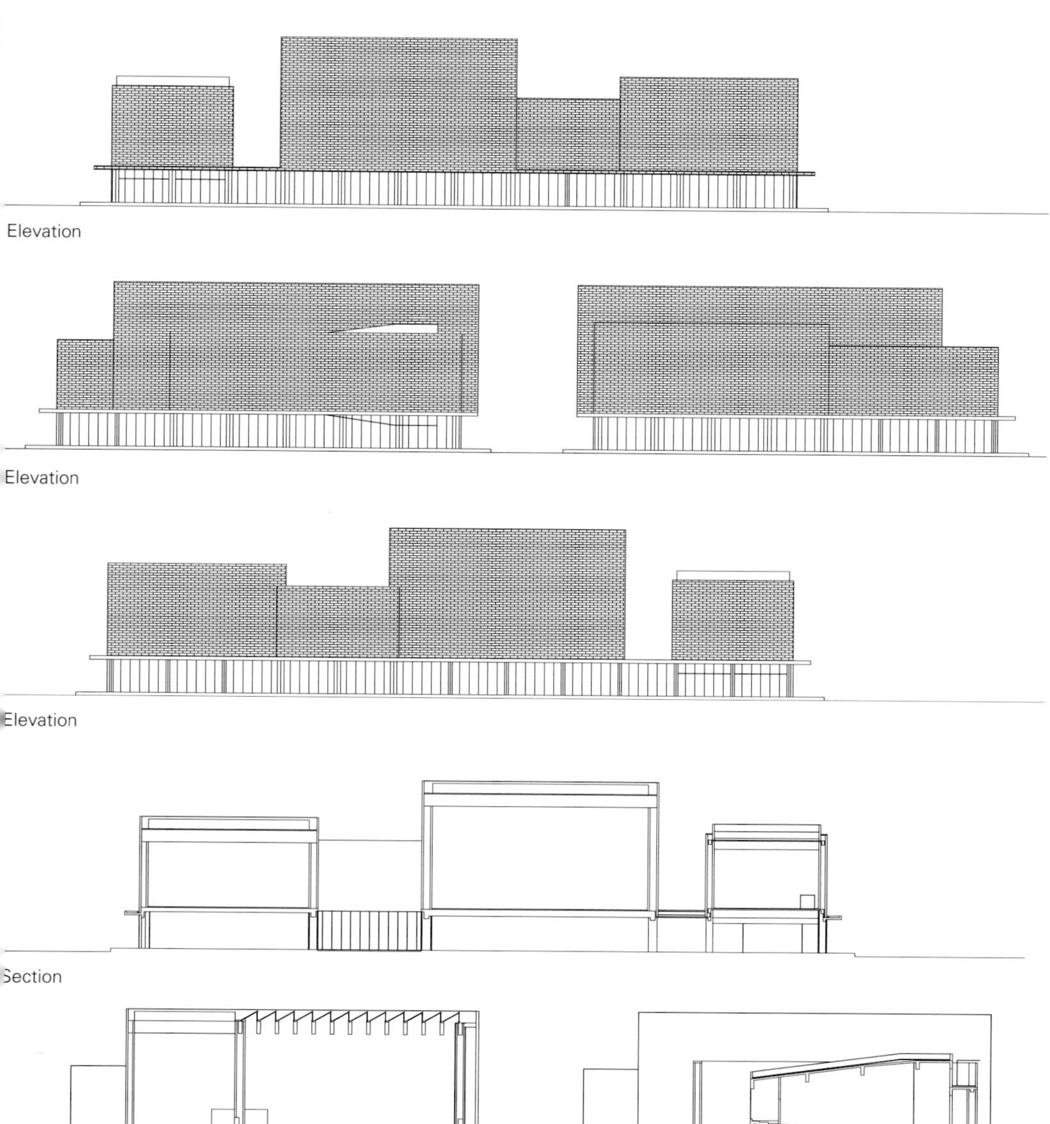

Elevation

Elevation

Elevation

Section

Section

Are you working on any projects outside China?

At the moment we're working on a gallery in New York City. It's a lot smaller than most of our projects here in China – the total surface area is only 400 square metres. But I'm told that's actually a very large project by Manhattan standards.

Culturally speaking, what is the relationship between your generation of designers and the previous generation of Chinese architects?

Many of them are still working, so I guess the two generations coexist independently. In terms of a working philosophy, I think you are inevitably stamped by your cultural background, but where you train is also a huge influence. On the other hand, I don't feel like I'm following a Western track or influence. Most of our projects are extremely low-budget and low-tech, so they are difficult to classify by Western standards. Our main priority at the moment is to improve the construction quality standards while working in a real-world environment, rather than on over-specified projects with large budgets.

Songzhuang Art Center is located in a small town on the outskirts of Beijing. Financed by a private developer, it is a public structure intended to cater to the burgeoning creative industries that characterise the area, transforming it into one of Beijing's creative poles. The building contains over 4,000 square metres of gallery space and other facilities

Ai Weiwei

ai Weiwei (Fake Design, Beijing)

ell us about the name of your office, Fake Design.

It's a little complicated. Several years ago my acountant came to me and told me we had to register company name for tax purposes. I made up a few ames for fun – silly names like Bed Works, Shit Dick, ussy Design and Fuck Design. The official in the deartment of taxation told me these words looked too oreign, but that Fuck would be acceptable because can easily be written in Chinese. It happens that in hinese 'fuck' spells out as 'fake', so our company ame turned into 'Beijing Fake Culture Development'. the West fake means false, so it's a nice double neaning.

What is Fake Design's design philosophy?

Keep it simple.

What projects have you completed recently?

Right around the corner there is a newly completd group of buildings, Courtyard 104 and 105, that says omething about my character. Even though it's only wo hundred metres away from my studio I never vised the construction site, or almost. I'm not interestd in what has been accomplished, work that has been uilt, neither my own nor that of others. I'm always lookg for the next thing – it's like an addiction. Once a projct is finished it's dead.

How long did it take you to design it?

I designed it pretty much in one afternoon. I didn't ink about it before that or after that.

You're saying you're not interested in the physical esult of your work?

Exactly. It's like a murder – when it's over, I need fresh body to kill. I'm not interested in dead bodies.

You're interested in the hunt.

I have a Swiss friend who's always inviting me to hunting with him. He tells me about the excitement I feel when I pull the trigger. I tell him I don't know… ou don't know until you do it, so I can't say yet.

What are you thinking about at the moment?

I'm almost fifty. I'll be turning fifty soon, and I have one so many things in my life that now I want to do ss. I want to rethink my life – maybe I should finish wisely.

Surely nobody's going to completely figure out what they should do with their lives.

No. But it's better to start thinking about it.

You wear many different hats. What distinguishes your design work, your architecture and your art?

As an architect, I spend most of my time dealing with the problems of the people who are going to use the architecture, how I imagine it will be used and how it reflects the identity of the user. When it comes to art you have to create a problem. You have to think in terms of art history, in terms of human visual imaginary, about relations, about man's aesthetic or moral condition. It's different from architectural practice, but on the other hand I've always thought of architecture and art as different theories with a single narrative. What at one moment seems very important later becomes a blur.

What is your relationship to Beijing?

This morning at 6am I went to the German embassy. I'm doing a project for Documenta 12, in Kassel, that involves transporting a large number of Chinese labourers to Germany for a few weeks. Each day I accompany a group of people to apply for a visa. Fifty labourers are allowed to present themselves at the embassy at a time, and I go along with them. I just got back from the embassy now, and on the way back I was thinking: I have absolutely nothing to do with this city except for its mental presence as the capital city of China, a political centre, the symbol of the Communist regime. I have family members and friends here, but apart from that this city has nothing to do with me.

How would your work change if you lived in the West instead of Beijing?

It's very hard to imagine. I think I would be much more abstract if I lived in the West. Problems would seem much more remote. The problems we face here are earthy, are tangible. We're at a turning point in our history.

Are you referring to China's long-term or short-term history?

I'm talking about our long-term history, although the past hundred years have been the most extreme. We were a colonial society that became a Communist

Courtyard 104
Architects: Fake Design, Ai Weiwei
Location: Beijing
Client: Mao Ran
Construction engineer: Fake Design
Site area: 3,044 sqm
Existing building: 1,322 sqm
Extension: 281 sqm
Structure: concrete, brick

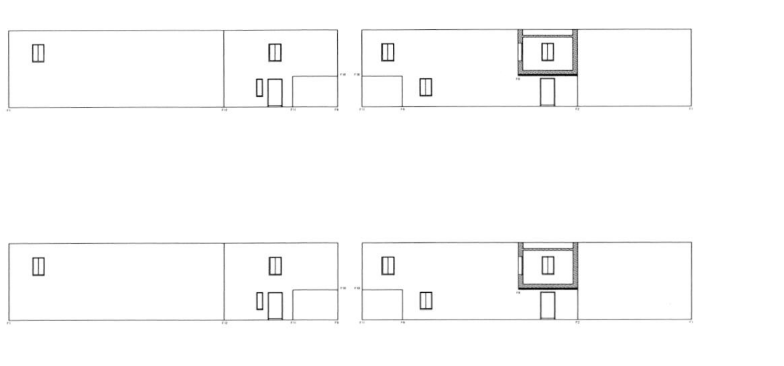

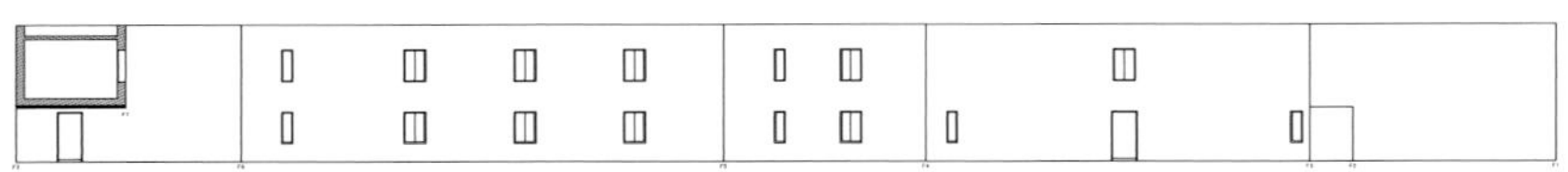

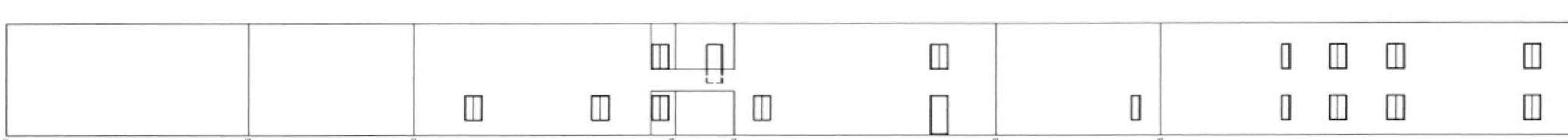

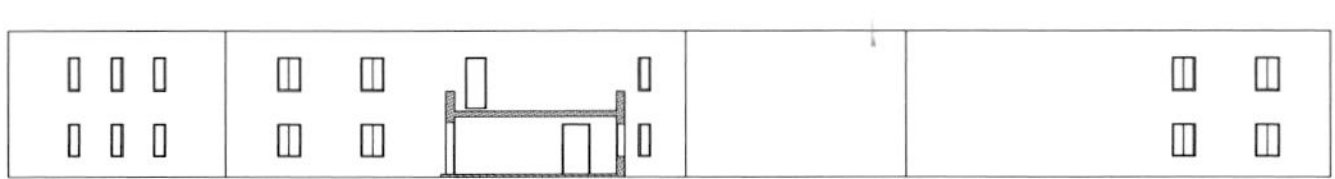

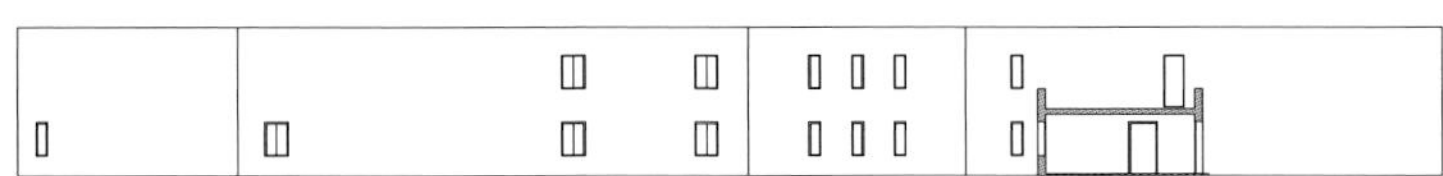

Unwrapped façade elevations

State and then a capitalist powerhouse. In a very short time we passed from agriculture to information age. It's quite exciting.

Yours is the only generation to have experienced both these eras. Do you have regrets about the path China chose?

It's like a fork in the road: you take one path or the other, and each leads to very different results. But after you've made your choice, history tricks you. It leads you to think: 'If I took the other path, everything would be totally different.' But I don't agree. There is such a thing as fate. Which makes it very hard to guess what's going to happen next. Too much calculation makes life simple and meaningless, less colourful, less imaginary. It shouldn't be like that.

In terms of your practice, is that sense of unpredictability and uncertainty necessary to your work?

It's absolutely necessary to me. You always feel better if your work doesn't look like the result of a bad habit, a duplicate of what you've done before. You often see artists copying themselves – it's so boring and senseless and meaningless. But it's a practice that is encouraged today.

Do you think of design in the same way?

Design is lucky because it faces a different set of constraints. In design, you have to solve a problem, and although the problem itself might be quite unpredictable, you get a temporary sense of satisfaction when you solve it. You feel a kind of momentary intelligence.

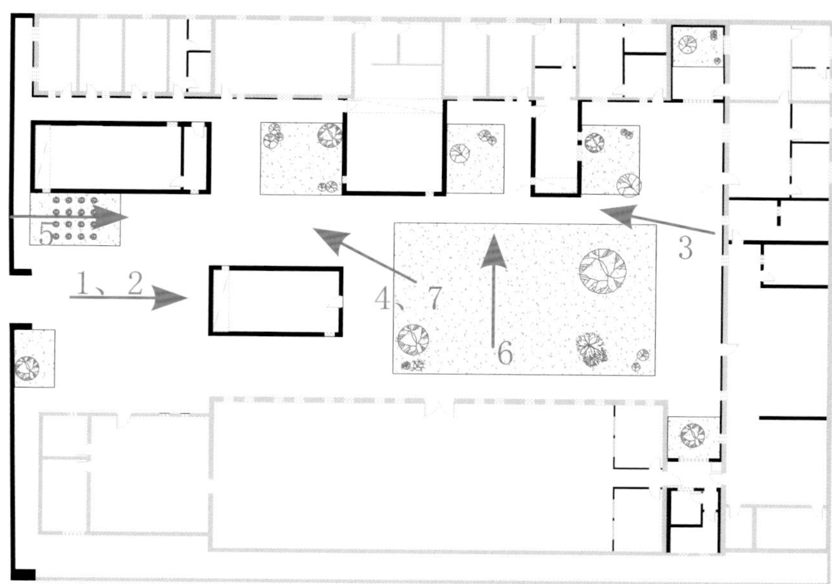

Site plan

Was there a period in history when people were designing in that way consistently?

Yes, I think in ancient Greece or during the Shang dynasty in China the individual's behaviour was less dictated by daily necessities. It was more spiritual in terms of its relationship with God – no, perhaps not God but another supernatural power. This resulted in a mode of design that addressed the permanent, universal human condition. Today 'efficiency', 'desire' and 'comfort' are the key words. That's why when we see design we often don't see intelligence.

Why did that change?

Life has become easier than it once was – societies are much more productive. Everybody can have a relatively pleasant, stable life, so there is less emphasis on spiritual being or spiritual becoming.

Do you think this has to do with a change in the way we perceive time?

Yes, I do think so. I believe society's perception of all the most fundamental dimensions – time, space, distance, volume – has changed, as have personal relations as a consequence. Anything bad is good, anything cheap is expensive. It's really upside down, inside out – and everything is still changing.

Do you think art is an indulgent practice?

Yes, I think it's indulgent, and indulgence onl brings self-destruction. Indulgence is unnatural. makes you an unbalanced person.

But do you think art is necessary in its supe fluity? Is it some kind of struggle with the desire f immortality?

Yes. I think any form of consciousness or u consciousnes is about that.

And architecture?

Good architects are very conscious of their mo tality and want to survive by proxy through their wor It's ridiculous but it's true.

Do you think Asia will find its own form of mode nity, a path distinct from Western modernity?

I guess what's so interesting about Asia at th point in history is that the time has come to answe that question.

It will be interesting to see whether, because c globalisation, it unquestioningly follows the West an appropriates its position. Alternatively, it might fin a new relationship to information, technology, u banism and so on. We'll see.

Opposite and following pages
Courtyard 104 and Courtyard 105 are two small groups of residential units in Beijing, each comprised of three double-level studio-houses that share a public courtyard while retaining individual outdoor spaces. The exterior walls consist 70% grey-coloured bricks and 30% red bricks. The design specifies simple construction techniques that leave the materials exposed on the interior

展覽 交流 培訓 實驗
空間分布：
展廳 多功能廳 工作室 看片室 書吧
音樂酒吧 餐廳 共享空間 樓頂花園

Pei Zhu

Pei Zhu (Studio Pei Zhu, Beijing)

How would you describe your practice?

Studio Pei Zhu is a young practice of about twenty employees based in Beijing. With our projects we try to explore methods of connecting the design process to the final product. The experimental nature of our work is influenced by the context in which it takes place – urban China. The recent rapid development of the country has created new urban environments that can certainly be described as 'modern', but lack the vitality and soul of older districts. One of our main concerns in design is to reconnect modern urban China to its roots, reinterpreting the vernacular in a contemporary context to create architectural devices capable of energising urban districts. In this way we hope to contribute to the creation of a regional version of contemporary architecture that blends with its local context.

One of your recent projects, Blur Hotel, deals with an interesting issue – the renovation of Communist-era architecture in Beijing's urban core. Can you say something about this project?

Beijing was once one of the best-preserved medieval cities in the world. Since 1949, however, the construction of government and industrial premises within the centre of the city has disrupted what used to be a free-flowing and non-hierarchical city plan through the construction of enclosed large-scale buildings placed without regard for the rhythm and consistency of the old city. The development of these 'tumours' within the ancient Ming dynasty core has resulted in the creation of a disjointed and incomprehensible city centre. In response to this problem, Blur Hotel, located on the site of a large government office beside the Western Gate of the Forbidden City, is an experiment in 'urban acupuncture'. Rather than operate and remove the tumour (in other words demolish yet again), a far less disruptive and violent method is to leave it in place and simply neutralise its ill effects. As a refurbishment proposal, the project aims to harmonise the existing building with its surroundings without resorting to backward-looking pastiche, and provide a beacon for renewal of the surrounding area. The first strategy employed with this end in mind was to open out the ground floor of the building to create a layer of traversable space occupied by public-oriented programmes. The next approach aimed to integrate the building more with the local building typology of the *sihueyuan*, or courtyard house. By simply carving into the concrete slab floors of the existing structure, an arrangement of alternating vertical courtyards was created replicating the spatial arrangement of the surrounding *hutongs*. With the interior of the building transformed, the third and final tactic dealt with the exterior, wrapping it in a continuous and semi-transparent façade. This skin is based on the image of a Chinese lantern and allows light in and out of the building on every floor, as well as diffusing its appearance into a uniform but permeable object.

Another of the buildings you designed, currently under construction, is a part of the infrastructure for the 2008 Olympics in Beijing. Can you say something about the Digital Beijing building?

The rapid development of the digital age has greatly impacted upon our society, our life and the urban realm. If the industrial revolution resulted in Modernism, what will the digital revolution result in? This is one of the questions we attempted to answer with this project. The Digital Beijing building is located on the northern end of the city's central axis and will serve as the control and data centre for the forthcoming 2008 Olympics. After the Olympics are over, it will accommodate a virtual museum and an exhibition centre for manufacturers of digital products. The concept for Digital Beijing was developed by reconsidering the role of contemporary architecture in the information era. The building is inspired by one of the omnipresent symbols of our age, the barcode, and will emerge from a serene water surface. The façade itself will resemble a circuit board, and the abstracted mass of the building will evoke the simple repetition of 0 and 1 in its alternation between solid and void. The idea is for the building to recreate the microscopic underpinnings of life in the digital age on a monumental scale. In the future, we expect it to be constantly under renovation as it evolves to keep pace with technology.

Blur Hotel
Architects: Studio Pei Zhu
Location: Beijing
Client: China Resource
Programme: business hotel and cultural facility
Building area: 10,176 sqm
Engineer: Beijing Zhongjian Hengji Gongcheng Co, Ltd

Following pages
Blur Hotel was born from the refurbishment of a decommissioned government office in a prime location near the Western Gate of the Forbidden City. Rather than demolishing the existing building, the architects chose to strip it down to the reinforced concrete skeleton and re-clad it with a permeable skin that diffuses the light at night

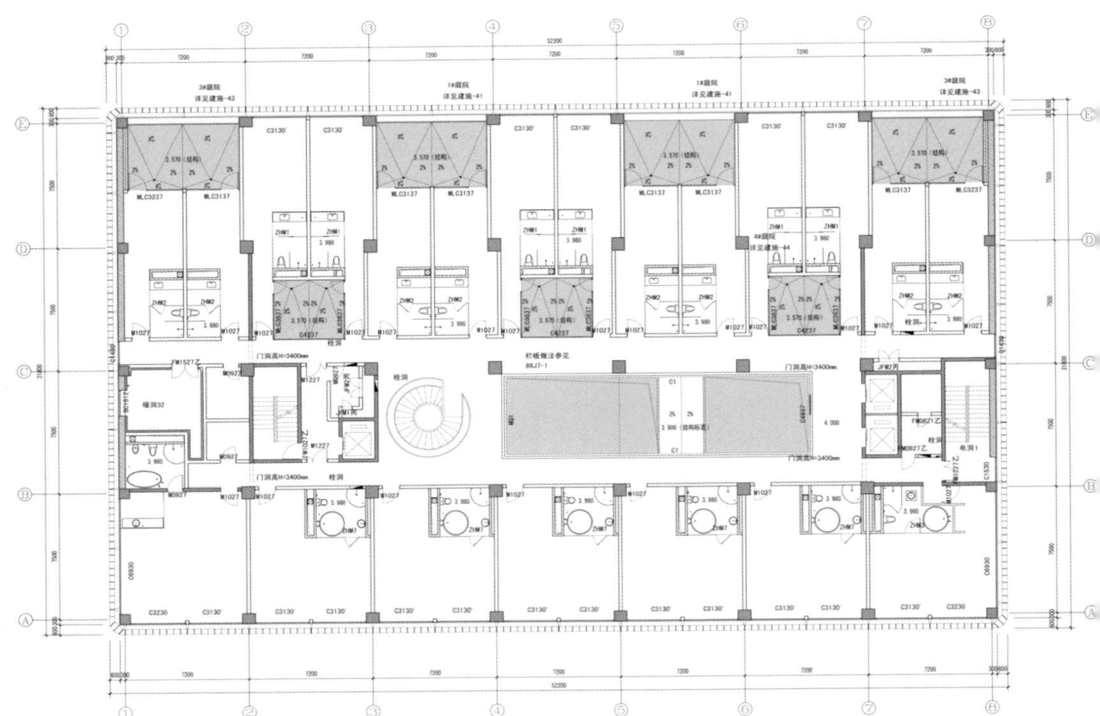

Second floor plan

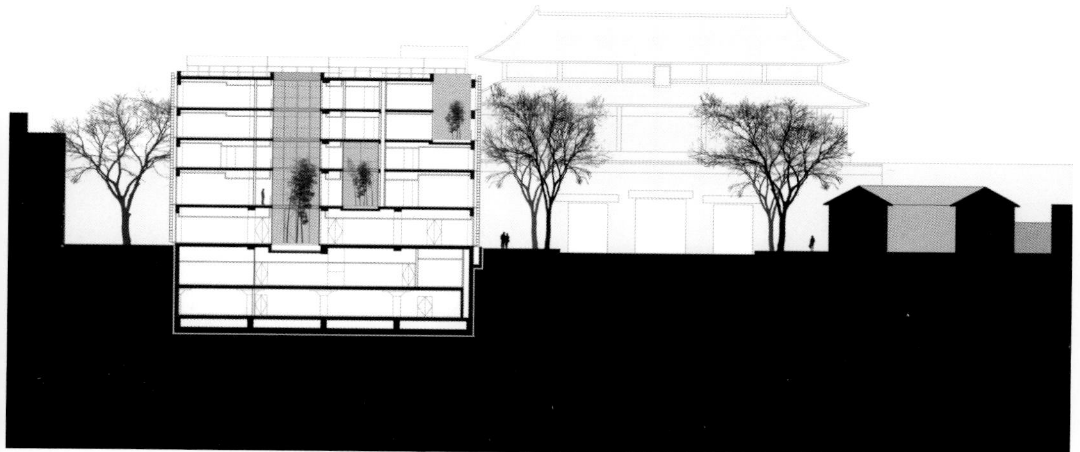
Cross section

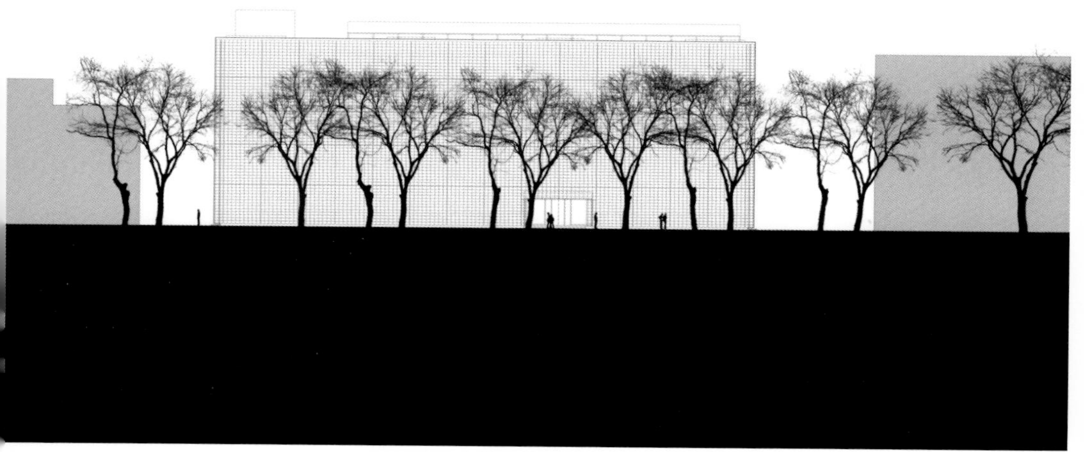
Longitudinal section

Opposite
The lobby of the Blur Hotel

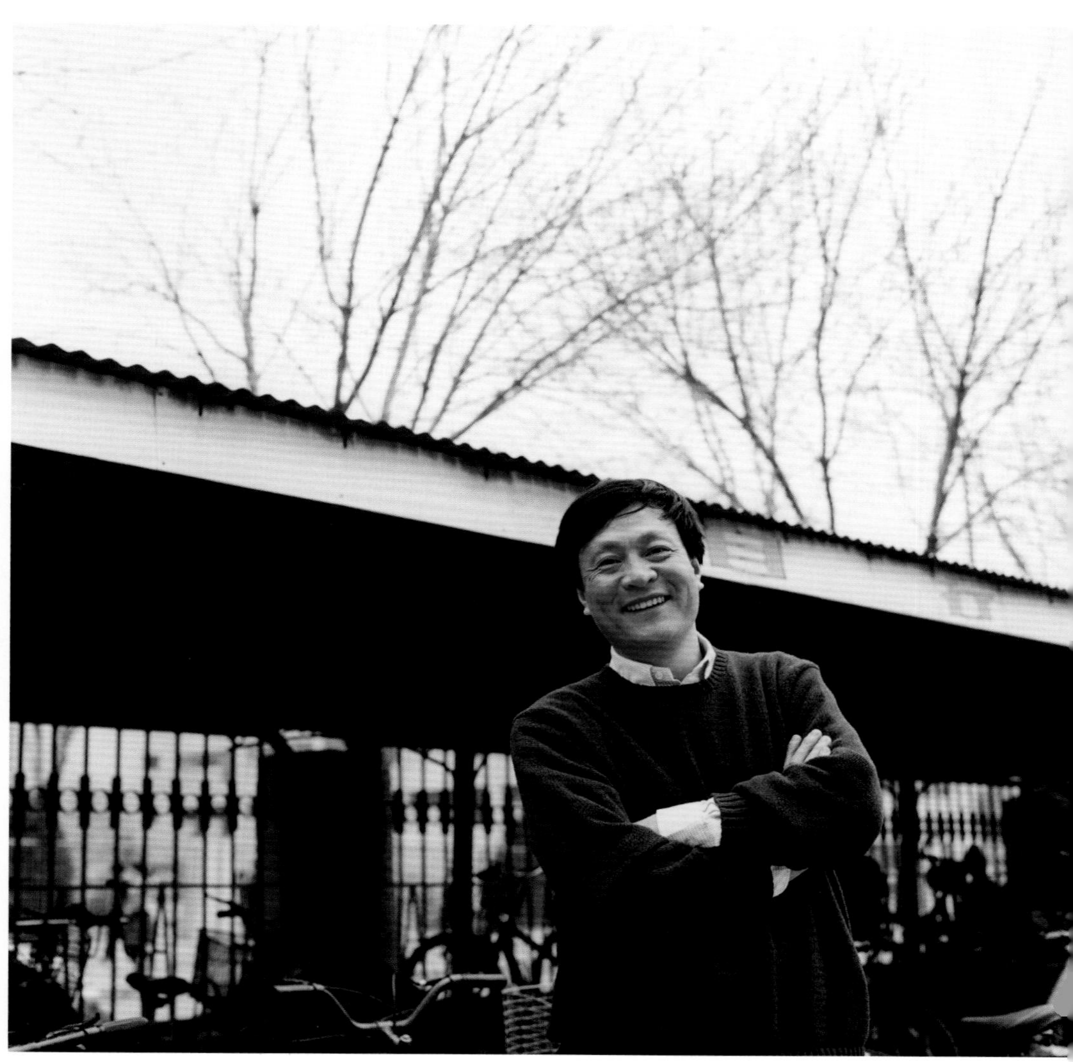

Kongjian Yu

Kongjian Yu (Turenscape, Beijing)

Maybe you could start out by saying something about the role of the landscape architect in China at this moment in time. Chinese culture has a very ancient and complex relationship with nature, but to say that this country's landscape is in desperate need of some form of thoughtful intervention is an understatement.

It's true. I think the potential of landscape architecture is undervalued in contemporary China. The subject is often discussed as if it's already 'too late', but that's not actually the case. Here in China we have even more to do than other countries precisely because the landscape is essentially all urban, all humanised, all developed. It's not like America, where one can still easily find vast wildernesses. Here every piece of land has been developed and cultivated for 5,000 years, and the government is continually rezoning farmland to make way for new urban developments. Virtually every piece of land will ultimately be developed, which means that every piece of land will need to be designed. Landscape architects have even more work to do than architects, but the paradox is that officially in China there is no such profession: traditionally the only landscape-related profession is that of the gardener. That will have to change soon. It's a sector that's expanding quickly.

How large is your practice, Turenscape?

We have three hundred employees and four different offices. On the face of it, there's no lack of work – we get a lot of calls from developers, government agencies and mayors from towns and cities across China. The problem we are now facing is that in order to be able to build decent projects you really have to do a huge amount of preparatory work in convincing and educating the client as to what environmental sensitivity is, what ecology is, what sustainability is. There's very little comprehension or education on any of these subjects in China at the moment. There seems to be a general misconception that what cities need right now are gigantic architectural icons. There's very little appreciation, even on the part of the 'experts', for architecture that has a humbler, more human scale.

How successful have you been in convincing your clients of the need for environmentally sensitive architecture?

It's pretty much universally recognised that the environmental issue has become one of the greatest challenges facing this country today. But the degradation of the landscape is now so widespread that the solution will clearly have to be driven by the political will to do something about it. On the whole, I guess there is an increase in the awareness towards these subjects. This afternoon, for example, I'm going to address a delegation of fifty mayors and try to convince them of the direction I think we should be going in. The central government is also starting to wake up to the environmental issues it will have to face in coming decades.

Is it at all possible to reconcile the infrastructural needs of an exploding economy with the principles of ecology and sustainability?

We will have to. That's why I call landscape architecture the art of survival. It's not an art in a decorative sense – it's about the survival of the nation. That's the landscape. It's a totally different way of thinking about how we should build. Traditionally 'landscape' meant gardens for collectors, for royalty, for the nobility, for the rich. Today that's a misunderstanding of the word. We are actually talking about life-or-death issues like designing our cities to be pleasant places to live, but also to withstand storms and natural calamities – or even wars.

You were telling us that Turenscape also designs masterplans for new and existing cities.

We base our large-scale urban planning around a strategy we call 'negative approach', which simply means we design the voids, the areas that will be occupied by the landscape, first. Cities spread organically, and if there is no infrastructure in place to preserve open areas they tend to devour public space and the existing pockets of the natural landscape that could be preserved. We try to consider elements of the ecological network such as water, fauna and existing settlements first, and then build cities around them. The issue of existing settlements is important. Villages are getting torn down every day to make way for the expansion of cities, without even questioning whether this destruction is necessary. In one of our recent projects we demonstrated that villages and even farms could be successfully absorbed into dense urban environments.

You returned to China from the US in the late 1990s. Was it a very different environment?

In the late 1990s the atmosphere was definitely much less open, and there were quite a few bureaucratic obstacles to working here after having lived and worked abroad. At that time you needed a professional certification that I didn't have, and it took me several years to get it. Also, there was very little understanding on the part of mayors and decision-makers as to the real potential of landscape architecture, so it was hard to get those first commissions.

One of the strategies of your practice is the principle of 'minimum intervention'. Could you explain this in relation to your Red Ribbon project?

The site of the Tanghe River Park is a river corridor at the outskirts of a rapidly expanding city, Qinhuangdao, in Hebei province. The area is rich in bio-diversity and lush vegetation, but over the years the site filled up with disused irrigation systems and dumped rubbish. What could have been an ecological sanctuary was destined to be engulfed by the outwards expansion of the real estate developments. The fields and the river would sooner or later have been replaced by channelled riverbanks and a shiny marble square, which is what had already been built on the adjacent section of the same river corridor. The challenge of this project was to protect the ecological integrity of the site while allowing the neighbourhood's inhabitants to use the site as an urban park. How could we preserve the natural habitat alongside the river while creating a new recreational area for the city's inhabitants? We took a decidedly 'minimum design' approach and proposed the construction of a 'Red Ribbon' that would weave along the river and lead into a willow grove. This ribbon would provide seating, lighting and orientation to the park's visitors, as well as making it safe for recreational uses like jogging, fishing and swimming. The Red Ribbon itself would be made of steel and would be approximately 500 metres long. The new park would cover an area of approximately 20 hectares. The project was realised, and the improvement in the riverside landscape was dramatic. This strategy was definitely successful in safeguarding the river corridor during the process of urbanisation.

What is the Red Ribbon made of?

The winding ribbon itself is made of steel and fibreglass and is lit from inside so that it glows red at night. It stands 60 cm high, its width varies from 30 to 150 cm, and it sits on a pedestrian boardwalk that appears to 'float' on the riverbank. Various plant specimens are grown in strategically placed holes in the ribbon. It's also important to point out that colour was a fundamental aspect of this project. Four perennial flower gardens (white, yellow, purple and blue) form a patchwork of colour on the park's open areas and turn what used to be deserted garbage dumps into attractions. The bright red colour of the ribbon itself lights up this densely vegetated site and acts as a visual connector between the diverse natural vegetation types and the four added flower gardens.

Opposite and following pages
The Red Ribbon is located in the Tanghe River Park, in the coastal city of Qinhuangdao (Hebei province). The park is situated in a 50-acre site on the banks of the Tanghe River, a derelict area previously earmarked for residential development. The main feature of the park is a 500-metre red fibreglass bench that winds through the site allowing passers-by to comfortably enjoy the riverbank. The bench, which was fabricated in local boat-building yards, contains recessed lighting fixtures that illuminate the boardwalk at night

Red Ribbon, Tanghe River Park
Architects: Turenscape
Design principal: Kongjian Yu
Location: Qinhuangdao City, Hebei
Project type: park, greenway
Owner & Client: The Landscape Bureau, Qinhuangdao City
Total site area: 50 acres

Qingyun Ma

Qingyun Ma (MADA s.p.a.m., Shanghai)

Unlike many other parts of Asia, where architecture practices generally adhere to a process of linear growth and progressive expansion, China seems to have bred an entirely new category of architects such as yourself who aren't afraid of starting out big. Over the last decade or so your practice, MADA s.p.a.m., has designed over one million square metres of buildings. Is it possible to design high-quality architecture in this context?

It depends how you define 'quality architecture'. If there's one thing you need to practice architecture in China, it's a lot of versatility and a considerable degree of ignorant audacity. The necessities of everyday practice inevitably require you to engage in the design of a vast assortment of building typologies, ranging from regional masterplans to small houses. Nothing here is as you would expect – even the growth pattern of a successful practice can be reversed, as it was in my case. We certainly don't feel threatened by this – on the contrary, we are nurtured and charged by it. We see this situation as an opportunity to discover new, unexpected and potentially revolutionary modes of practising architecture.

Can you give us an example of what you mean?

Normally in the West, a practice starts small and grows progressively larger, but in China we have successfully experimented with a reversed pattern, from huge to small. The practice starts huge by 'putting plenty of dishes on the table', in other words engaging in the large-volume commercial work that is only too easy to come by here. It's like an obese person who decides to get back into shape – you start out big and keep exercising until you get fit. It's a common Chinese belief that it's much easier to find one's optimum size through a process of reduction rather than expansion. Growth can lead to an irrational, uncontrollable obsession with bigness, ultimately resulting in inefficiency. What I'm trying to develop is a cutting edge suited to cutting not one but many things. The portfolio of my office spans from urban development strategies (such as the Shanghai North Bund Development Strategy) to urban redevelopment design (Ningpo Bund), urban design (Huzhou New Urban Centre), urban megastructures (Tianyi Center, Xian TV), right down to tiny buildings and interiors such as the Father's House project.

My philosophy is that a knife can be sharpened for one thing by cutting another. It is true that complexity, magnitude, multiplicity and an excessive appetite are not qualities sophisticated society or good manners encourage, but it's interesting to point out the obviousness of something that took the architectural profession in the West more than fifty years to realise, in other words that diversification is a key to business success and a necessity to survival. Our portfolio might be huge, energetic and unclean, but it's a true-to-life reflection of contemporary China's large, diverse and chaotic society.

In the massive thrust for expansion and densification currently underway in most Chinese cities, public space is often preserved only in the context of commercial activities, malls and retail-based neighbourhoods. Is there anything that can – or should – be done about this?

The relationship between public space and commercial activities is a very pressing issue in China at the moment. One thing that is often left out of the discussion is the issue of 'use', or more precisely, informal use by people, because public space is only qualified as such through popular use. 'New urban space'

Following pages
Father's House in Lantian (Xian province) was designed by Qingyun Ma as a rural retreat for his father. Built entirely by local labourers, it is largely constructed out of materials found on the site such as smooth river stones and rocks from the nearby mountains

Father's House
Architects: MADA s.p.a.m.
Location: Lantian
Site area: 200 sqm
Total surface area: 385 sqm

Client: Peijie Ma
Exterior contractor: Zongqi Fan
Interior contractor: Shanghai Dumiao Interior Decoration Co, Ltd

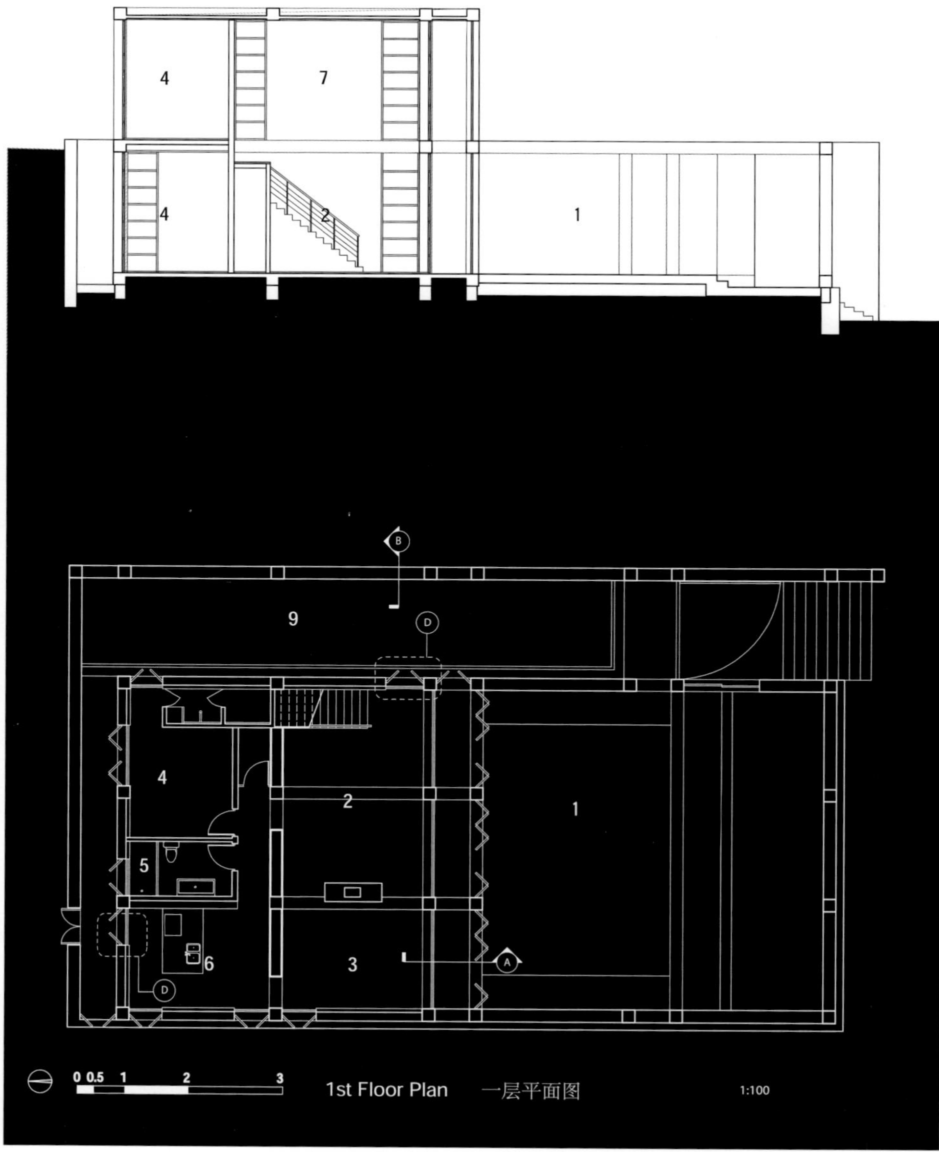

1st Floor Plan 一层平面图 1:100

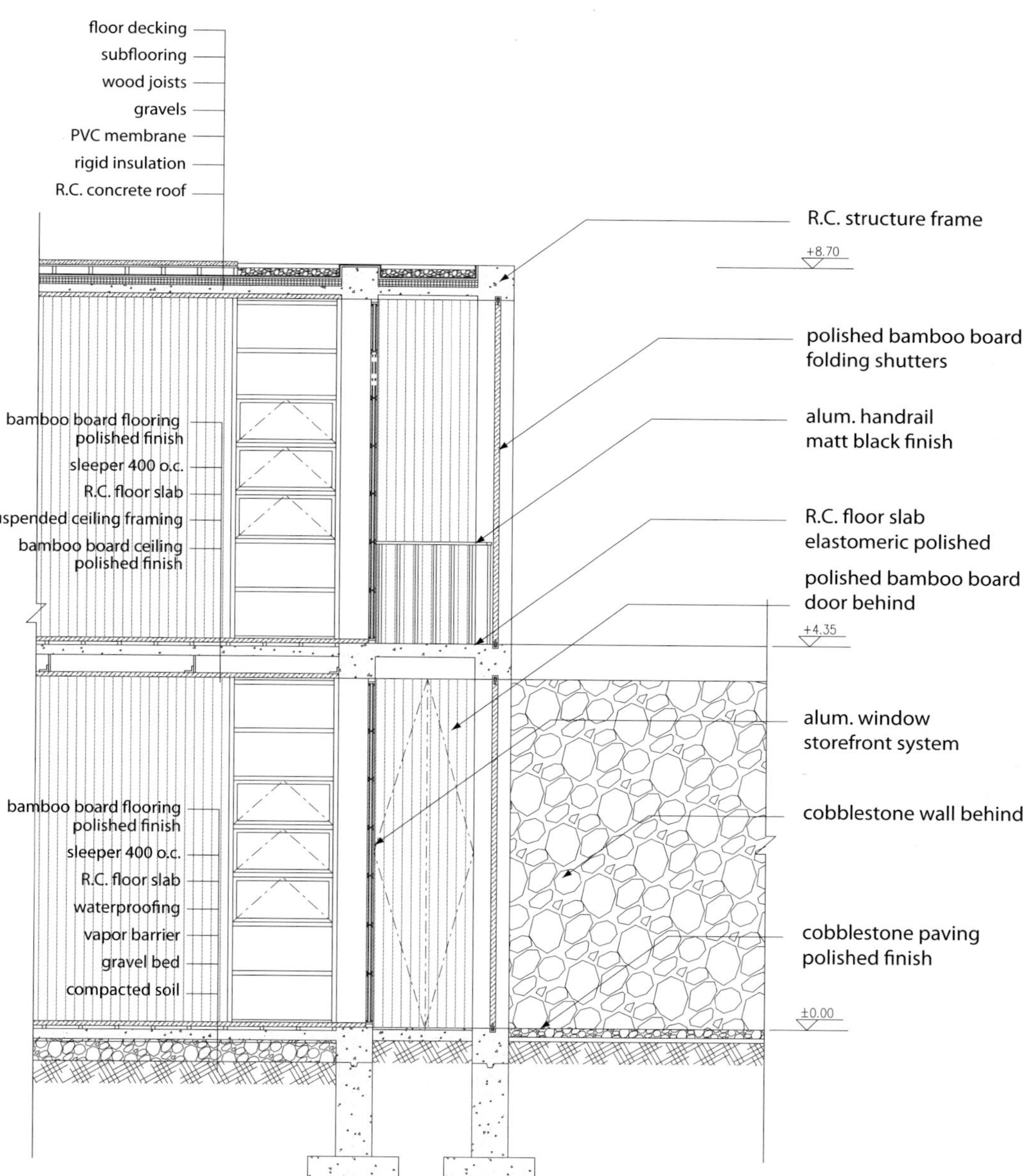
floor decking
subflooring
wood joists
gravels
PVC membrane
rigid insulation
R.C. concrete roof
R.C. structure frame
+8.70
polished bamboo board
folding shutters
alum. handrail
matt black finish
bamboo board flooring
polished finish
sleeper 400 o.c.
R.C. floor slab
suspended ceiling framing
bamboo board ceiling
polished finish
R.C. floor slab
elastomeric polished
polished bamboo board
door behind
+4.35
alum. window
storefront system
bamboo board flooring
polished finish
sleeper 400 o.c.
R.C. floor slab
waterproofing
vapor barrier
gravel bed
compacted soil
cobblestone wall behind
cobblestone paving
polished finish
±0.00

Construction diagram

in China often indicates space poorly equipped with both urban commerce and public spaces. I worked on two different commissions recently that approach the problem from opposite angles, both of which were successful. In one case, Thumb Island, the building was a 'public space' supportive of or supported by commercial activities, whereas in the other, Snake Street, it was a private commercial development that effectively functioned as public space through the continual presence of people. I think both are valid formulas, if they engender public use. The problem is that in China these kinds of spaces often end up in the hands of a popular new profession called 'commercial consultancies' which homogenise everything into cubes with simple but meaningless dimensions and bleach all colours into a whitish beige, deadening the public space in the process.

What is your lowest-budget commission to date?

Probably the Library of Zhejiang University. The rationale behind the commission was brutally clear: education facilities receive among the lowest levels of funding on the national financial planning scale. What China still does best are straight lines and perpendicular corners, and if there are constraints of time and cost, the language of architecture is inevitably reduced to these most basic elements. Our building largely employs the two cheapest materials to be found locally: red mud brick and orange fir wood. It's not a refined building, but the fact that it only took eight months to finish with an overall budget of $160 per suqare metre makes all the other subtler notions disappear. MADA's own office in the centre of Shanghai was also an extremely low-budget project. Due to time and budget constraints, we simply re-clad an existing concrete shell that used to be a Red Star kindergarten in the 1970s with woven bamboo board.

At the other end of the dimensional scale lies F ther's House, a poetic countryside dwelling in Lantia

Father's House is a country retreat I designed an built for my father in his hometown. Geographically, it an interesting location: Jade Valley and the Qinglin Mountain Range meet there to form a spectacular bac drop to the site. They define the whole territory with vastly changing landscape, from steep mountainsides t mild slopes and rivers, eventually evening out into an e tensive plain called Middle Plateau. Father's House res in the ambiguous position between the river and th mountains, both of which offer an abundance of buil ing materials. The first and foremost principle of the de sign was to maximise the use of local stone and loc construction methodologies. To simplify the constru tion process we minimised the non-local labour and ove all mobilisation required, so the use of alien materials suc as concrete remains a minimal and distinct elemen whereas use of the local materials such as stone an wood is maximised. The river was our source of roun stones, and the mountain of coarse stones. We used lo cal manual labour extensively during the building proces and kept the construction technology extremely simpl The house's external panels alternate between concen trations of dark and light hues, rough and smooth te tures, reflecting the richness in variety of the stones t be found nearby. The building's shutters are made ou of the same compressed woven bamboo boards I use on the exterior of our office in Shanghai. Since I first dis covered this extremely cheap material on a building si about five years ago, it's become a favourite. It's usua ly employed to make concrete formwork, but I think it actually got huge potential in other uses and can be ver beautiful. It works particularly well in this project be cause the collision of rough, organic materials with th measured and spare forms of the concrete frame give the house an ephemeral, deeply Chinese quality.

uch of the interior is lined with
ompressed woven bamboo panels, an
expensive material normally used to build
rmwork on construction sites

ıe courtyard is protected from the harsh inter winds of Lantian by a stone wall. 'hen the building is occupied, the bamboo-ınel shutters can be folded aside to reveal veeping views of the valley below

Controlled Explosion
A Conversation with Jiang Jun

For several years Urban China, *the magazine you edit, has meticulously and painstakingly collected, archived and divulged observations on the processes of transformation that cities across China are undergoing today. As one of the most knowledgeable observers of Chinese urbanism, what do you think sets this country apart from other nations that are experiencing rapid metropolitan growth, and more specifically, do you think anything can be learned from what is happening in China today?*

A lot of comparisons are being drawn at the moment between China and other countries, but I think what is really unique to China is its 'city-making' process, and more specifically the absolute dominance of the government in this practice. Historically, there is actually a tendency in this direction all across Asian countries and civilisations. A key premise to this is that the State is the sole landowner, which in turn leases it out to individuals, companies or developers, usually with a long-term leasehold contract. This is actually a strategy for financing construction or expansion: even quite small or poor cities can raise expendable capital by auctioning off vast leaseholds, which they in turn can reinvest in infrastructure and public buildings. It's like making a 'nest' for the developers, who can then spark off a development boom. This is what we call 'planned capitalism' or the 'planned market economy', where capitalism and individual initiative can be bred within a premeditated framework. It's very similar to what Keynes referred to as 'national capitalism', in which the State itself resembles a large enterprise that has the goal not only of maximising profits but also of protecting the best interests of the population.

This is only within the framework of the city. If we look at the macroscopic, multi-regional scale of the Special Economic Zones in the south-east of China (especially Shenzen but also Shanghai, Pudong, the whole Yangtze River Delta and most recently Tienjin), State government has absolute control not only through the possession of land but also through the imposition of a strictly regulated masterplan. The development of these special zones occurs through a process of 'monocracy', a combined planning and economic strategy in which all the major players are gathered by the State into one specific site. In this way, the government can focus its developmental efforts on a relatively restricted area and more easily retain control. In the 1980s it was Shenzen, in the 1990s Shanghai, and now it's Tienjin.

What you are describing sounds like an urban planning scheme on the scale of an entire nation. Could we say that this was the result of an extremely centralised process of 'economic masterplanning' that continues right up until today?

Yes, to some extent that is the case. Sometime around the end of the 1970s Deng Xiaoping spoke explicitly of China as having two parts, one being the East and the other the West. He established that the East should develop first, and specified that this development should be fully complete by 2000, after which the East would support the West during its period of growth. His forecast was, in general, quite accurate. Together, the PRD (Pearl River Delta), YRD (Yangtze River Delta) and Bohai Ring are actually one of the four major sectors of China, constituting the south-east part. The second sector is the north-east area, the third is the south-west with its centre in Chongqing and Chengdu (a key area in terms of experimenting with a new type of economic zone that attempts to integrate the city and the countryside), and the fourth zone is centred around Wuhan.

Could you say something more about this characteristically Chinese urban entity that you described, i.e. the government-owned, government-designed city?

It would actually be a mistake to overstate the control the government has over the city. It's an issue of scale: the government is the planner, not the architect, in that it sets out the framework within which private enterprises physically shape the city through single buildings. The State's position used to be closer to that of the architect, trying to control every detail, but most of that is today done by developers: what we have nowadays is a form of controlled *laissez-faire*, in which the free economy has infiltrated parts of the framework, but control of the overarching parameters is retained – and tightly guarded – by the State.

How does the architect as a professional figure fit into this scenario? I read that during the years of the Cultural Revolution there was no word for architecture as an occupation, and that design professions were marginalised to the point of exclusion. In the following decades there seems to have been a progressive return, to the point where today China is the biggest market for architectural services in the world.

At first architects were almost solely employed in the government departments of planning. The architectural profession was very closely linked to the idea of 'caring for the people', so it involved a lot of designing social housing, factory cities and public buildings. Even today there are many nationally controlled architectural design institutes directly or indirectly owned by the government, although in some instances they have partially merged into the market economy, mostly through stock market flotations. In these instances the company's shares are owned by the State, which also appoints the company's CEO. This is a characteristically Chinese business typology, run like a private enterprise but in essence no different from the governmental planning departments. These offices only account for one third of the picture, though, as there are another two typologies of architecture practices operating in China at present. The first is comprised of the large international offices, and this set in turn has two subsets: the 'hyper-efficient' corporate firms like SOM, KPF, RMJM, etc., and the 'stars', such as OMA, Zaha Hadid and so on. The latter set might not have large numbers of staff, or build very many square metres, but they are hugely influential because of their enormous visibility in the media. The third typology is a group we refer to as the 'returned Chinese students'. These are Chinese architects who travelled abroad to study, usually in prestigious international schools of architecture such as the AA, Harvard or Columbia. Qingyun Ma, Urbanus and MAD are all examples of this type. They represent the voice of a growing local power constituted by independent, privately-owned practices.

I believe it's important to say a bit more about the role of the State-owned design departments, as big changes are occurring there at the moment. They still have a position of quasi-monopoly in the market, especially because large international companies are allowed to practice in China only on condition that they partner with one of these State-owned design institutes. In addition to this, there is an increasing tendency for them to proliferate by setting up 'sub-offices' run by lower-ranking partners of the departments. Some of these design companies have as many as ten smaller offices, each practising under the name of a single architect, some more famous than others. The aim of these 'fake freelancers' is to achieve a more personally-oriented approach to the design process, while remaining under government control. This means that actually the government, through a network of offices, is still almost completely in control of the market, especially when it comes to housing and public buildings, which of course is a largest market in China by volume, and also one of the most profitable.

Much of China's phenomenal urban growth has, both in environmental and social terms, come at the expense of the country's rural areas. What is the relationship between the city and the country in present-day China? Is there a future for a post-agricultural countryside?

There was a period in the years before the 1980s when the countryside was intentionally sacrificed for the benefit of the cities. The household registration system assigned groups of peasants to tracts of State-owned land, which meant peasants were essentially prisoners of their villages, and couldn't leave them under practically any circumstances. The major problem of the Chinese villages was overpopulation: there was too little land and there were too many people, so during the 1980s the land usage system was reformed and land use and land ownership were separated. Ownership was still collective, but the use of the land was allocated to individual families, so that excess manpower from the countryside could overflow into the city without disrupting the social structure. At this very time cities were undergoing a construction boom, so a large segment of the rural population migrated towards the urban centres to join the labour market in the construction of the city or the manufacturing of products along the coast. The driving force of urbanisation was undoubtedly the labour borrowed from the countryside through processes of mass migration and relocation.

It is estimated that another 500 million people will move from the country to the city in the next few years, and this explains why the price of real estate in the cities is escalating so rapidly. There's no hope of this changing unless the government intervenes in the market by means of a massive injection of social housing.

The social and economic differences between the city and the country appear today to be such that one could almost describe rural and urban China as two separate countries. Is anything being done to address this divide?

When Hu Jintao took power in 2003 there was a substantial shift in strategy – his style of government was very different from that of his predecessor, Jiang Zemin. He introduced the concept of 'Harmonious Society', according to which the various sectors of the country should advance together and assist each other in the process of development. The richer areas that benefited from rapid growth in the 1980s and 1990s, in particular, should support the development of the weaker and poorer ones. It was into this context that the 'Socialist New Village' (a plan to revitalise the smaller towns across China) was born as an official State strategy. Agricultural taxes were abolished, and a lot of subsidies were redirected from the cities to the countryside, shifting the emphasis away from the creation of megapolises in favour of actually supporting extra-urban development.

How does the figure of the urban planner in China compare to that of his or her Western counterparts?

The most obvious difference is that in Western countries it is perfectly normal for an architect such as Rem Koolhaas to design masterplans. In China, on the other hand, architecture and planning are kept strictly separated because urban design is not only a financial and fiscal instrument for the State, but it is also a macro-balance tool for the civil economy. The spatial structure of the city is actually the dominant power behind the development of China: modernisation goes hand in hand with urbanisation. Most of the benefits of this process of development have the potential to directly affect the careers of the professionals involved in the urbanisation process such as developers, urban planners and so on. So, to avoid corruption and retain control, urban planners operate exclusively as part of the government. This used to be true of architects as well, but nowadays they have achieved a much greater degree of detachment. Planning is still unquestionably a monopolised sector of the market here.

Is there any sign of this situation changing? Is the urban planning profession heading towards a more liberal market?

There is a move in that direction, but it's slow and anything but straightforward. There are several private companies splintering off from the urban planning institutes while remaining under their umbrella so as to share the benefits of being both part of the market and part of the government. If you consider the planning of a zone, a street or even a town, then the day when that will be freed into the market is in sight. But if you move up in scale to the regional plan for land usage, the macro-planning of a city, or the design of a megalopolis in the PRD, that is still strictly government monopoly and there's no way a private planner will get that kind of an assignment any time soon. On a popular level, there is an increase in the subjective, 'unprofessional' interest people are taking in urban planning issues. It's something I've noticed among contributors to *Urban China*. It's especially true in the richer cities where there is a nascent bourgeoisie. By 'unprofessional' I mean common people without specific training who can talk about the city from their own perspective. It doesn't matter if it's an anthropologist, or a dramatist – they can always talk about the city because the city's organisation affects their daily lives, and they are actually starting to understand this in its full significance. If we talk in professional terms, however, a 'real' urban planner needs to understand and design the spatial structure in economic terms too. This makes planners a highly specialised professional body, and this could become an obstacle to communication with the outside world. *Urban China* is very interested in stimulating discussion between professional and non-professional groups – we like to think of ourselves as an interpreter and conduit between the policy-makers and the general public, or at least representatives of the public, in the hope of improving the situation as much as possible. There's actually a very interesting trend towards an increase in public participation in the decision-making processes in China at the moment. This is true particularly in Shenzen, which was one of the first cities to achieve relatively widespread wealth. A certain degree of middle-class self-organisation is actually being encouraged there now, as a kind of consultational experiment. Urban planners and urban planning institutes are opening themselves up more and more to consultation.

What position do the universities and schools of architecture occupy in the scenario you outlined?

Institutions like Tongji University and Tsinghua University are very powerful, particularly on the organisational side. They integrate education, production and research into a single entity. They are very much based on a practice-oriented educational system thanks to which students are given the opportunity to get involved in the real-world city-making process alongside their professors. Tongji University, which recently celebrated its 100th anniversary, is becoming more and more important as a centre for the creative professions and the culture industry, both fields the national government is putting more and more emphasis on. These universities are becoming incredibly successful hubs of modernisation and are usually surrounded by industrial parks, high-tech parks and other very profitable businesses.

The university system is, presumably, a stronghold of the government. How do you see it evolving in the coming years?

Universities are the fortress of ideology, so of course there's no question of privatisation. Even foreign universities like Harvard and Columbia have been barred from setting up permanent branches here. Some run 'workshops', which is essentially the most they can do until they are granted 'certification'. The universities are the ultimate pillars of ideology, and the government is very much aware of their importance. On the other hand, many other types of barriers have been raised. People are now allowed to travel abroad to study, and many can actually afford to, so this is already weakening the grip of the government on the youngest generation. Some smaller, less famous universities have succeeded in opening branches here. The university system was actually the subject of a hypothetical proposal we formulated in a recent workshop in Shenzen. Our proposal was for a new Special Intelligence Zone (modelled on the Special Economic Zones of past decades) somewhere on the border between Shenzen and Hong Kong. This project would host a special university co-sponsored by the Universities of Shenzen and Hong Kong under the auspices of the Ministries of Education and Sciences: it would be a kind of virtual academy where universities from across the globe could open branches and operate in a condition of pseudo-freedom. It's just an imaginary project, but it raises questions as to the possible effects that could be achieved if the education system were opened only slightly. Think about the remarkable effect that the small opening towards Hong Kong had on Shenzen's economy; and imagine the potential of replicating something like that in the field of education.

Jiang Jun is a Beijing-based designer and critic. For several years he has been working on urban research and experimental study, exploring the interrelationship between design phenomenon and urban dynamics. He founded Underline Office in late 2003 and has been the editor-in-chief of *Urban China Magazine* since the end of 2004. His works have been presented in international exhibitions such as *Get It Louder* (2005–07), Guangdong Triennale (2005), Shenzen Biennale (2005–07), *China Contemporary* in Rotterdam (2006), Kassel Documenta (2007). Born in Hubei in 1974, he achieved his bachelor's degree at Tongji University in Shanghai and a master's degree in Tsinghua University in Beijing. At present he teaches at the Guangzhou Academy of Fine Arts.

SOUTH KOREA

Minsuk Cho

Minsuk Cho (Mass Studies, Seoul)

Today South Korea is one of the world's most powerful economies, a stunning turnaround from the war-torn, impoverished Korea of the mid-twentieth century. How has the nation's rapid industrialisation affected the development of a new architectural identity?

I believe there's a struggle going on in the minds of the younger generation, particularly at this moment in time. Over the last decade a large number of young architects returned from the US and Europe and started practices here, and have just begun to receive significant commissions in the last few years. This is inevitably causing us all to pose ourselves the question: what is 'Korean-ness' at this moment in time? What is our relationship to tradition, to the architectural identity of this culture? In a way, I think my generation has answered this by saying: Let's just forget about that for a minute. The changes that have occurred over the last fifty years have been so unimaginably profound that any attempt to invent some kind of regionalist architectural style would be inevitably smack of artificiality and affectation. Korean architecture of the past developed in a context that is so far removed from today's reality that the whole operation would be pointless. That's not to say that we should blindly follow Western architecture – what I mean is that we need to develop a new form of Korean-ness, more spontaneous and more responsive to today's hyper-dense, media-saturated reality. For myself, a turning point in understanding this was Rem Koolhaas' research project on the Pearl River Delta. It inspired me to understand architecture and urbanism as something more than an issue of aesthetics: it's the meeting point and expression of countless social, political and cultural forces, so as the forces at play change, architecture must change with them.

At what point do you think South Korea's architectural consciousness changed?

Probably the early 1990s. It was a period of unbelievable optimism. Korea's economy was booming, and for the first time it actually felt like a wealthy, modern, industrialised nation. We were one of the richest countries in the world, and could afford to invite the world's best architects to build here. Pretty much all the big-name architects of that period had projects in Korea. Then came the economic slump of 1997 – what we call the IMF Crisis – and most of these schemes were cancelled. Very few survived, among which was Rem Koolhaas' contribution to the Samsung Museum of Art (Leeum). I was assigned to work on that: it was my first experience of working on a real architecture project in Korea.

You studied at Columbia University for three years, worked for various practices in the US and Europe, including OMA, and then set up your own office in New York with James Slade. What made you return to South Korea?

I left New York in late 2001, shortly before the attacks on the World Trade Center. Despite the incredible optimism that permeates the city of New York, it's a difficult place for an ambitious young practice to work. Everyone dreams of building from the ground up, not simply carrying out endless refurbishments. So when we were commissioned to design a house *ex novo* on the outskirts of Seoul, I decided to continue my partnership with James Slade but move part of the practice back to Korea. It was a time when the idea of the networked office seemed truly possible to realise, and the likelihood of accessing larger-scale commissions was decidedly greater in Seoul. And if you think about it, Seoul is a great place to base a practice in Asia. Tokyo, Beijing and Shanghai – some of the largest and densest cities in the world – are all one and a half hour away. We carried out two projects as an international partnership – Pixel House and Dalki Theme Park. In the two years we worked this way, it became increasingly evident that there was a lot more to the design process than simply e-mailing pictures and drawings back and forth, so in 2003 James and I decided to go our own ways. It was at that point that I founded Mass Studies.

Seoul is very different from New York. How did this change of context influence your work?

At the moment Korea is probably the Asian country most committed to pushing the limits of high-rise architecture, in every sense. In Seoul, for example, you'll find lots of high-rise towers that contain either cineplexes or shopping malls, and for that reason have no windows. High-rise buildings are something Mass Studies is becoming increasingly involved in. We designed our first high-rise project in 2005 (Boutique Monaco, currently under construction), and it got considerable attention from developers. Since then the office has grown from four to thirty-six employees. But

NER
DELI

Opposite and previous pages
Ring Dome is a temporary pavilion built out of 1,100 white hula-hoops and 10,000 nylon zip-ties. It was designed by Mass Studies in 2007 to celebrate the 25th anniversary of Storefront for Art and Architecture, a gallery in New York City

the reality of working in Seoul is actually a lot more complex. I don't think there's another city quite like it. Seoul is taken by the market economy to the point of obsession, and everything, including personal relations, is quantity-driven – for example, the kids of people who live in a 200-square-metre apartment don't hang out with kids who live in 100-square-metre apartments. Everything is about numbers, quantities and brand names.

In some respects Seoul is Hilberseimer's dream come true. The city is largely constituted of apartment blocks, massive slabs often arranged like walls flanking Han River or the main arteries. It's really like something out of one of Hilberseimer's renderings. Here urban living unequivocally means apartment living, and although they're cramped and not particularly attractive, apartments in central neighbourhoods can cost several millions of dollars. We call them 'chicken coops' – microscopic dwellings that you have to work all your life to earn. 90% of all new buildings are apartment blocks, and apartments, just like everything else, are brand-name commodities. Samsung, Daewoo and LG all make apartments and stick badges on the outside, just like on cars. Another amazing thing about Seoul is that there is so little space that the suburbs are just as dense as the city. In Western cities, the architectural typologies you find in the suburbs are completely different from the centre. Here you find the same highrise blocks right up to the city limits – the only thing that changes is the location. So you can understand how exceptional and satisfying it was to be commissioned to design Pixel House from scratch. From the developer's point of view, Seoul has been so successful that it has become a point of reference for other 'up and coming' Asian cities. China, Vietnam, Kazakhstan and other countries undergoing rapid urbanisation have all taken Seoul as a case study, and entire cities are being slapped together out of the box on the model of Seoul. Part of the reason for this popularity is the 'Korean Wave' phenomenon. Since the 1990s, Korean pop culture has been exported all over Asia – soap operas, TV programmes, pop music and advertising are some of our largest industries. Asia's pop culture factory used to be Japan, but now even Japan watches Korean programmes. Korea is somehow considered a nice, digestible, Westernised take on Asian culture, and is safer and more appealing than its Chinese equivalent.

South Korea is a place where a large number of very complex realities intersect, and this usually manifests itself in the cities. Korea is 82% urbanised, compared to a global average of 50%. It is predicted that the global average will only reach 80% in 2030, which puts us twenty-three years ahead. It is one of the hardest-working countries in the world – apparently we work 60% more hours than the Dutch. There is massive social segregation, with a lot of the apartment blocks acting as vertical gated communities. All this has led to a real breakdown of the social fabric, with half of all marriages ending in divorce and negative growth rates of the population. People just don't want to have kids because it's so stressful, expensive and competitive.

Have any of your projects sought to directly engage the incredible complexity and stratification of the city?

Several have, but one project in particular takes on Seoul's idiosyncratic social mechanisms. It's called Digital Flaneur. An interesting thing about Seoul is that it's actually possible to live in the city without owning anything. If you give up the bourgeois dream of living in the Hilberseimer chicken coop, you can live a perfectly decent life as a homeless person. There are innumerable capsule hotels, bathhouses, Internet cafes, gyms and entertainment halls for which you can pay by the hour, 24 hours running, and they're not expensive. Access to a bath-house costs $10 per day, which even includes yoga classes and celebrity performances. Of course you still have to make a living, but that's also possible. In Seoul you can survive on a completely contract-free job – there is this slow courier service that uses public transportation instead of motorbikes or bicycles; it takes a bit longer but costs the customer half as much. A lot of pensioners make money this way – all they need is a mobile phone and the ability to carry up to three kilograms.

Can you tell us about Oktokki Space Center, completed just a couple of months ago?

The client for this building is the most important architectural model-builder in South Korea. His work

shop has sixty employees. I met him when he built the model of Dalki Theme Park we exhibited at the Venice Biennale. His private obsession is with space, spacecraft, rockets, satellites and so on. Over the years he has accumulated an unbelievable assortment of models of all sorts of craft, and even travelled to the US to get information directly from NASA. He actually built one-to-one replicas of some of the Apollo spacecraft. Eventually all these models were shown in an exhibition in Seoul. It turned into such a big hit that he decided to build a permanent exhibition hall for it, and commissioned us to design it. The intention is for it to not look like a building at all. The lower part, the exhibition hall for the models, is darkened so as to create the illusion of being in space. The tower has an observation deck at the top, with a view of the surrounding area and a telescope for looking at the stars at night.

Previous pages
The Oktokki Space Center is an aeronautica theme park situated on an inclined site spread across 15,000 square metres of lanc on Ganghwa Island, located in an estuary of the Han River. The Center is comprised of educational exhibits and indoor/outdoor interactive facilities for children, focusing or space science and space aeronautics

Opposite and following pages
The site is dominated by an observation tower surmounted by an astronomical observatory; a winding staircase connects the tower to the main exhibition spaces

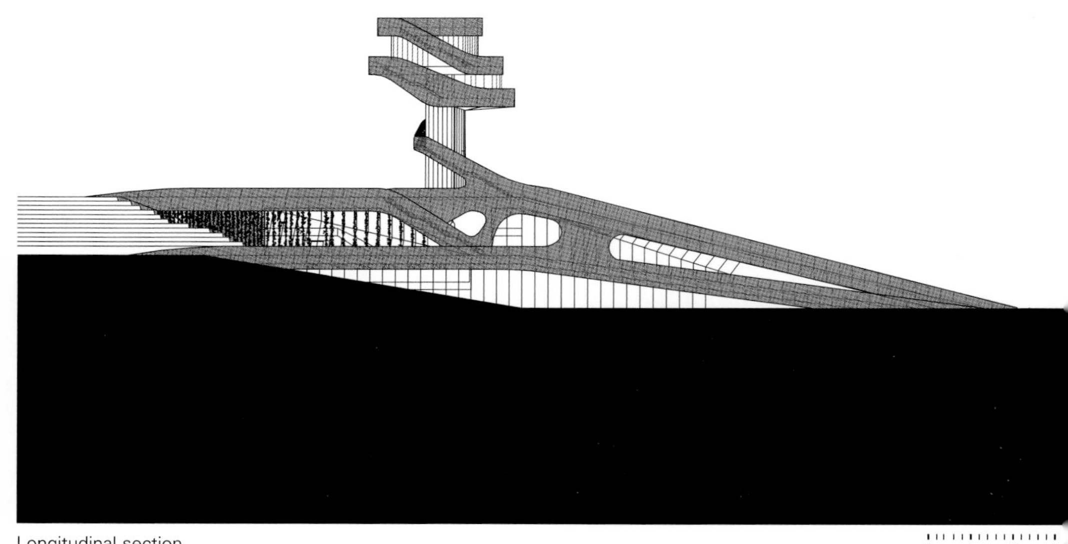

Longitudinal section

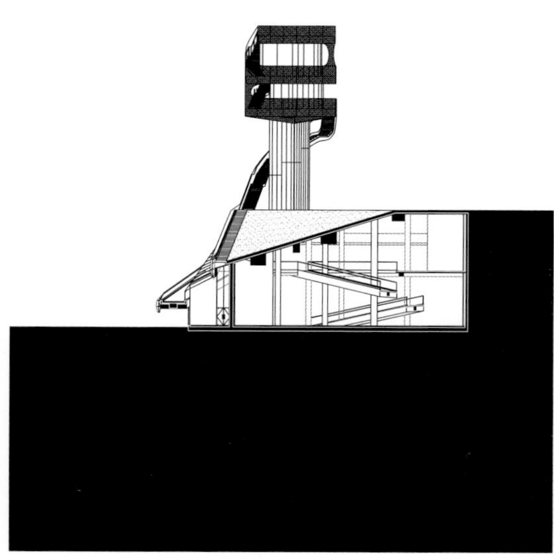

Cross section

Oktokki Space Center
Architects: Minsuk Cho + Kisu Park
Design team: Mass Studies
Location: 1026-2 Duunri, Bureun-myeon, Ganghwa Island
Site area: 14,854 sqm
Gross floor area: 1,748.25 sqm
Total floor area: 4,736.91 sqm
Floor area ratio: 13.98%
Structure: reinforced concrete
Finish: stainless steel mesh

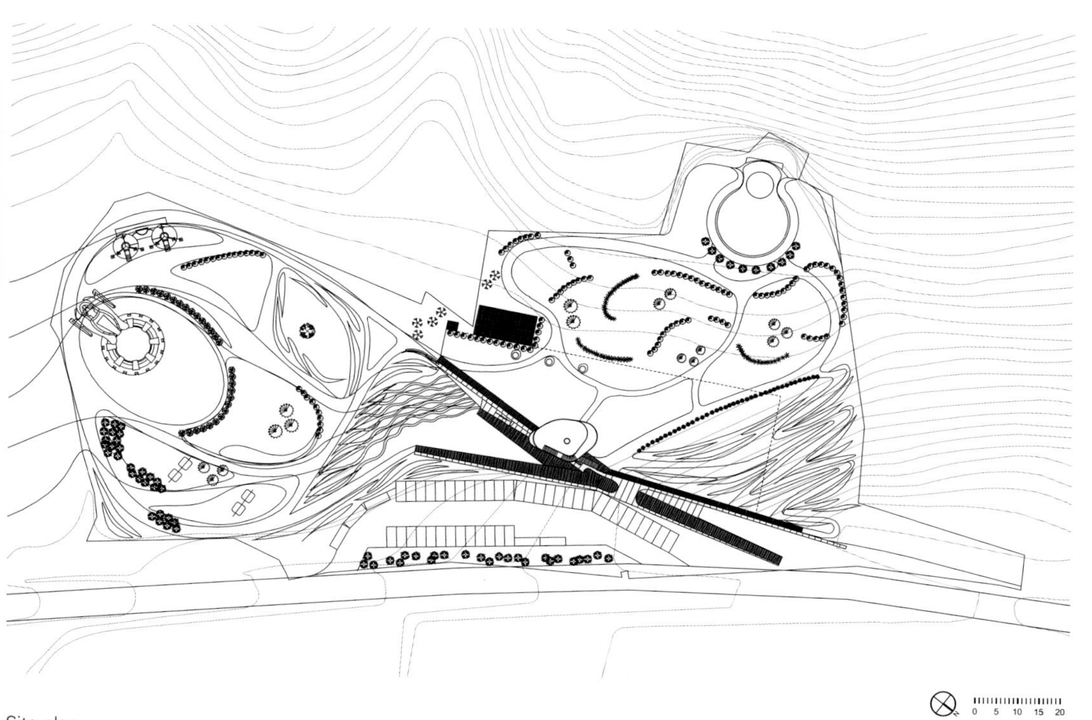

Site plan

Moongyu Choi

Moongyu Choi (GaA Architects, Seoul)

Unlike other Korean architects of your generation, who at some point practised in European or American offices, you worked for Toyo Ito in Tokyo in the early 1990s. Despite their proximity, South Korea and Japan seem to share very little in terms of architectural culture. What did you bring back from this experience?

On a very practical level I learned to work with a much lighter and more ephemeral kind of architecture. In Korea we're used to working with quite heavy elements like brick and concrete, and Japan introduced me to a much lighter palette of materials, such as steel and wood, that are used frequently there because of the seismic vulnerability. I've often used hybrids of these two palettes in my buildings. Japan also gave me quite a different perspective on the design process – it triggered off a process of thought through which I became very uninterested in architecture as form-making, and more concerned instead with using each project that passes through the office to develop specific ideas or to tackle specific problems. Returning to the issue of foreign influences, in a recent interview published in the architecture journal *C3 Korea* Spanish architect Daniel Valle said that he thinks my buildings have a lot in common with the work of the Dutch. Even though that may be the case, I think it's a mistake to evaluate a designer on the basis of forms rather than his or her ideas.

Can you give me an example of the ideas you are working on at the moment?

I've been working on a design process called M3, an approach through which the spatial requirements for a given programme are evaluated three-dimensionally and not simply in plan. It seems obvious, but if you think about it the vast majority of buildings are constituted of identical slabs stacked vertically, usually as close as possible. This is especially true here in Seoul, a city dominated by high-rise condominiums in which apartments are bought and sold on the basis of their area, not their volume. In many parts of Europe, you'll find apartments with ceilings of various heights – the ones with higher ceilings might cost more per square foot, but on the other hand they might suit some people's needs better. Here in Seoul the issue of volume is never even discussed, so you have no option. M3 is a proposal to think about space differently, to find alternative ways of accommodating programme within buildings by understanding the space three-dimensionally. Since I opened my office here in 1999, I've done a lot of work looking into the way space is used in Korea – right down to really simple issues like the way apartments are laid out.

What is your generation's relationship with writing and architectural theory? Does it define your practice in any way?

Not nearly as much as it defined the work of the generations prior to ours, in particular of architects born in the 1940s. I think they really felt the weight of their duty to somehow theorise the relationship between the Korean vernacular and Modernism. It caused them a lot of stress and preoccupation. It's a stage that other rapidly developing countries such as China and Indonesia will have to go through too. For better or worse, my generation is much more emancipated and takes a more intuitive approach towards architectural problem solving. More than in architecture, I think there is the need to develop a better theoretical understanding in urbanism. Cities here are developing so rapidly, and no-one really has a proper understanding of how a city of twenty million people should work, be it inside or outside Korea.

Paju Book City and Heyri Art Valley have given you and many of your colleagues the opportunity to build and experiment, but they are far removed from the reality of Seoul. 90% of all new buildings here are apart-

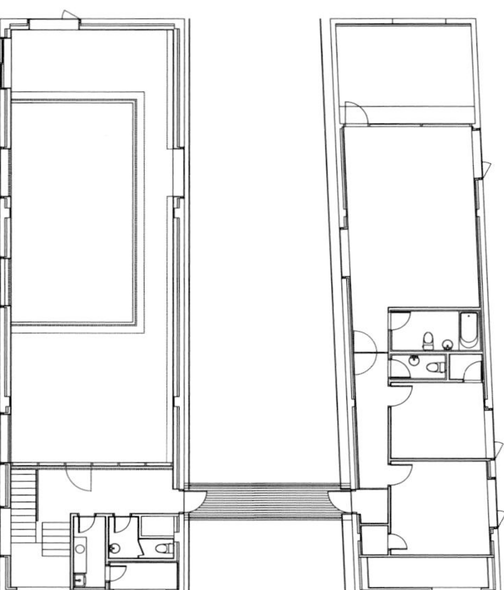
Fourth floor plan

TaeHakSa Publishing House
Architect: Moongyu Choi
Client: TaeHakSa Publishing
General contractor: LJ-Tech Construction
Location: Munbalri, Gyohaeup, Paju
Site area: 1,025.7 sqm
Building footprint: 441.67 sqm
Gross floor area: 1,626.95 sqm
Structure: reinforced concrete
Exterior finishing: exposed concrete

TaeHakSa Publishing House, an editorial office building located in Paju Book City on the outskirts of Seoul. The upper part of the building was partially completed and left empty to accommodate for the future growth of the company

First floor plan
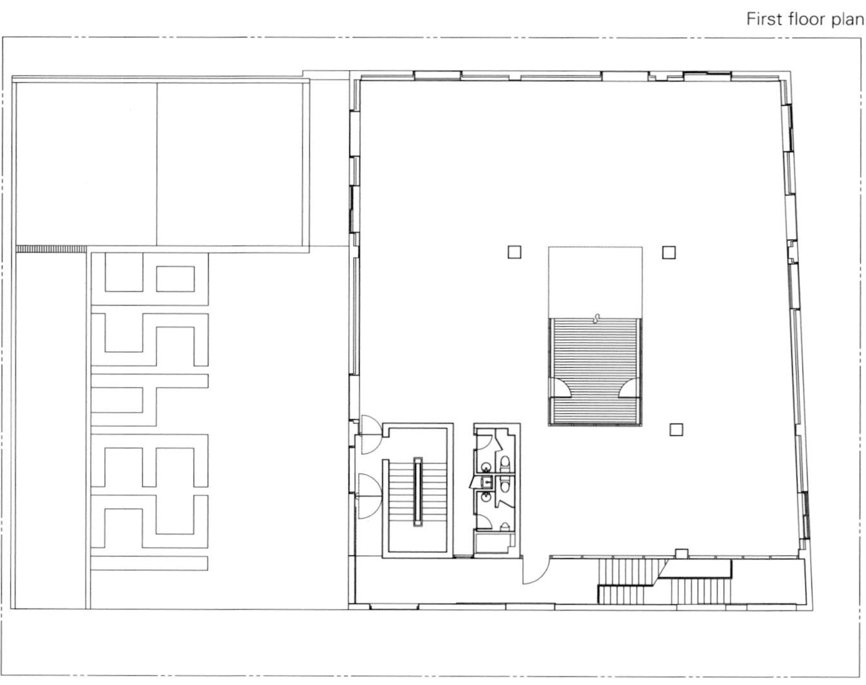

태학사

Following pages
Booksea Publishing House, Paju Book City on the outskirts of Seoul. The building's L shape is dictated by Paju's construction guidelines to preserve the view across the site

ment blocks built by developers. Have you had the opportunity to work with developers at all?

Unfortunately, not many architects get the opportunity to work with the developers who are really building the city around us. Most of us have worked on public buildings, dwellings and a few constructions in Paju and Heyri. These two are, as you imply, slightly idealistic, slightly removed from everyday reality. In a sense, they were incredibly successful in that they gave an entire generation the opportunity to cut their teeth on real-world construction projects. But in another sense they became architects' showrooms, the setting for a generational beauty contest. I think the time is right for a different kind of conversation to start happening – my hope is that over the next five years we'll be able to develop a more complex and articulated engagement with the city.

Are you optimistic about the city's future?

I'm very optimistic for the future of Seoul. It's much cleaner and safer than it once was, and the economy is booming. If anything, the problem is that it's going too well – the price of real estate is growing so quickly that many young people have no way of buying a house here anymore.

One of the critical issues in Seoul as in many cities with vibrant market economies, is the scarcity and gradual decline of public space.

I have an interesting story that illustrates the situation quite well. A couple of years ago, we designed a small retail complex in central Seoul. The building was to house a few dozen shops, but instead of enclosing them in a mall we arranged them along a spiralling walkway that wrapped around a public, open-air courtyard. We named the complex SamJi Street because it was configured like a street wrapped in a spiral. It became an extremely popular meeting place. So much so that the owner decided to start charging admission just to be able to access the courtyard and the shops. At that point there was a public outcry – people started demanding to know why it was called a street if it was not open to the public. After a week the owner was forced to open the doors again. This story is very indicative of the pressures facing public space in a city like Seoul – even in commercial districts. I think the architect is a very important mediator in this battle for space – it's something that has never really been discussed seriously in Korea up to now.

When I was born in 1961, the average per-head income was $80 per year. Now it's $20,000. In situations of rapid growth things get left behind, and one of these is public space. A period of adjustment is needed. Urban expansion moves unbelievably quickly – just thirty years ago, the southern part of Seoul didn't even exist, and now five million people live there. That part of the city was built almost overnight, and the last thing the developers worried about was the quality of public space, or issues of social or environmental sustainability. Today expectations are different, and it's something the city of Seoul is going to have to face.

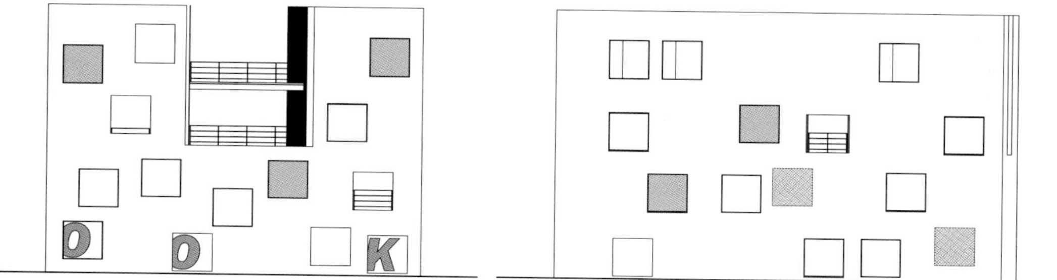

East elevation

North elevation

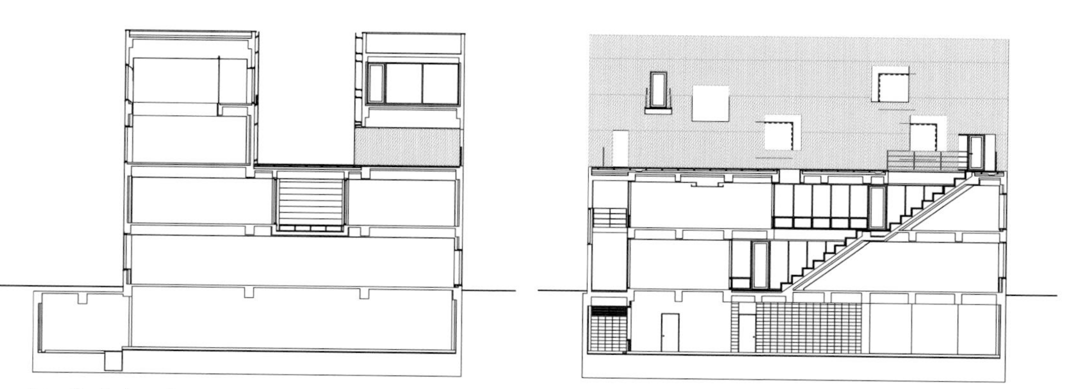

Longitudinal section

Cross section

Gallery io
갤러리아이오
Bookhaus Publishing Co.
서 해 문 집
파란자전거
Blue Bicycle
태학사
5655
3123

Yoongyu Jang

Yoongyu Jang (Seoul)

Can you tell us about Gallery Yeh, one of your most recently-completed designs?

Gallery Yeh is a seven-floor mixed use building in one of Seoul's more fashionable neighbourhoods. Its primary function is an art gallery – this takes up the two lower floors. The other floors are mainly comprised of offices and workshops.

What were your intentions with the design?

The intention behind the Gallery Yeh project was to create an enormous urban canvas. If a typical canvas can be thought of as a two-dimensional medium, the canvas we have conceived for the gallery is the spatial skin developed out of the new relationship we have found between the floor plan and the three-dimensional volume. We gave the two-dimensional attributes of the gallery wall the opportunity to deform into space. This process amounts to searching for a new type of space that lies somewhere between the folded façade and the smooth, continuous skin of the opposite wall. We call this a 'skinscape'.

How would you define the term 'skinscape'?

A skinscape can be initiated simply by acknowledging the urban fabric surrounding a building as a force acting on the envelope. 'Skinscape' can be best described as an experimental term resulting from the conceptual union of the architectural skin and the loose meaning of the term 'scape'. It is the variable result of the union of skin and other elements, layers or programmes of a building. Skin plus structure, skin plus space, skin plus programme and so on. The inevitable result is a physical deformation. The process of determining the appearance of a building is itself governed by the concept of skinscape, and it is possible to maximise the variations that emerge by carving away the excessive spatial elements or adding on more spatial 'fat'.

Following pages
Five vertical bands of concrete undulate as they climb the façade of Gallery Yeh, creating fissures that regulate the amount of light that reaches the building's seven floors, two of which are occupied by exhibition spaces. Residual areas on the upper levels are rented out as offices and artist's studios. As one of the tallest buildings in the neighbourhood, Gallery Yeh has come to represent a landmark in the area, reinforcing its reputation as a pole of the arts within Seoul

Publishing house in Paju Book City

Hailim Suh

ailim Suh (Himma, Seoul)

our practice, Architecture Studio Himma, designed wo of the most distinctive publishing houses in Paju ook City. Although there are substantial material dif- erences, they are both characterised by a fractured, al- nost kaleidoscopic appearance. Can you tell us about ne design process behind these two buildings?

As with most of my architecture, both these build- gs are shaped and influenced by a process of in- estigation and interpretation of the given site. I start- d by carefully considering what would be occurring these places – a fundamental objective was to es- blish a dialogue between programme and envelope. oth buildings are on Bookmakers Street, the main ar- ery of Paju Book City, and were designed in con- nction with Junsung Kim of hANd Architecture.

Borim Publishing House produces books for chil- ren, and the assigned programme was comprised of ne company's editorial offices and a marionette the- tre for children. The offices are housed in two verti- al slabs clad in perforated metal screens, and these abs are in turn intersected by the horizontal slab of ne marionette theatre. The theatre's undulating out- r shell evokes an idea of movement through space, ke the body of a puppet gliding across the stage. ust as the puppet's feet are always slightly elevated om the floor, the theatre floats a few feet off the round, at the eye level of children.

The House of Open Books was commissioned by publisher specialised in the translation of foreign ooks, particularly philosophy. The initial intention was construct two buildings on the site, one for the ed- orial offices and the other for the translators' apart- nents. The two buildings were shaped by the sight- nes crossing between River Han and the mountains. ne of the fundamental ideas behind this scheme is at in translation the two languages are like parallel nes – they appear to converge at the vanishing point, ut they never actually meet. It's an illusion, and the ame is true of languages. Translation never can be per- ect. So the building's circulatory system is organised rough a series of ramps that continually expose you lines that appear to converge in the distance. The xternal shell, in particular, is shaped by a number of naginary vanishing points that give the illusion – but nly the illusion – they can be reached.

Over time the brief changed considerably because they realised they weren't going to be able to get translators to move out to Paju Book City on a permanent basis. At that point the client decided, to my horror, to change the programme of one of the buildings first into a wax musuem, then into a furniture gallery, but refused to change the architecture in any way, which didn't really fit my ideas about programme-driven design...

The complex fractured geometries of these buildings suggest an interest in digital design processes. Do you consider yourself a digital architect?

Actually, no – I don't consider myself part of the digital generation. I studied under John Hejduk at Cooper Union in New York in the late 1980s, and that was a very important turning point in my career. He placed huge importance on experimental techniques of representation, many of which were extremely labour-intensive and involved long nights of drafting. I think that period was one of the high points of pre-digital draughtsmanship. We did these huge drawings entirely by hand with lead pencils: extremely subjective representations of the flow of the body in space and space in the body, forms that could capture the subtle fluctuations of movement... These are some of the things I see in digital architecture today, but we were doing it by mapping the body – I guess it was very specific to that particular moment at Cooper. I had an almost obsessive interest in the skin, acupuncture points, all the organs and how they are connected. I guess my real aim was to chart what exists but is invisible. That period influenced my approach to the whole design process for many years to come.

In what ways, besides the graphic techniques you learned?

John Hejduk was probably the most inspirational professor I ever had. The message he taught me was that you have to seek the kind of space that can bring out your cultural background. It was quite a revelation for me: I left Korea for the US when I was fifteen, so my education was entirely Western. I studied classical architecture and postmodernism with Bob Stern at Columbia, and spent some time at Harvard GSD as a student of Rafael Moneo; but Hejduk was the one who

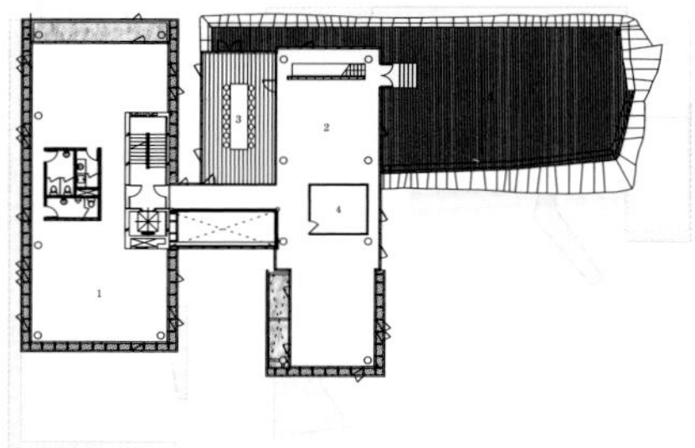

Third floor plan

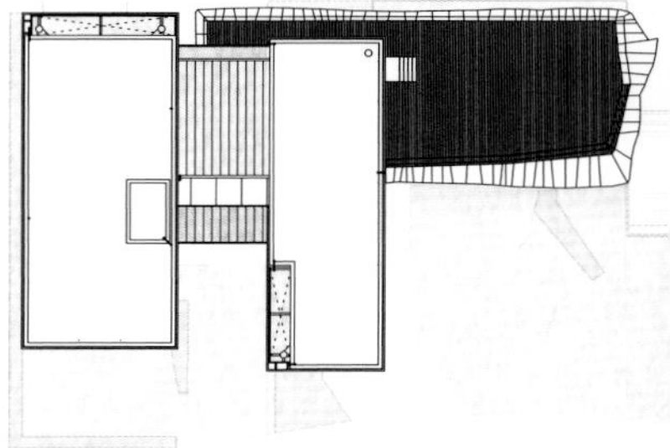

Roof plan

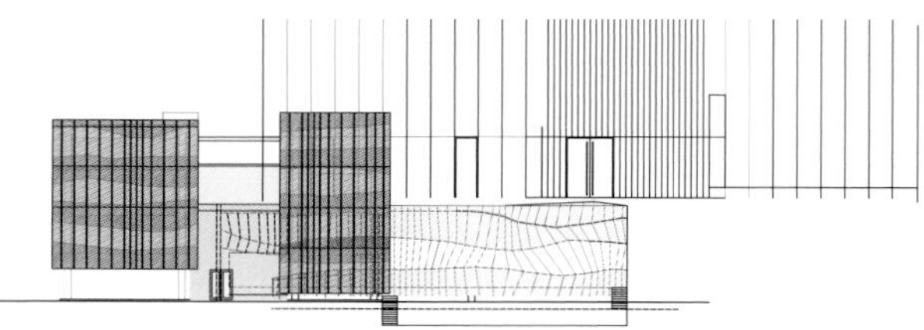

Elevation

Borim Publishing House and Marionette Theatre
Architects: Hailim Suh + Junsung Kim (Himma)
Location: Gyohaeup, Paju
Site area: 1,720.5 sqm
Gross floor area: 2,878 sqm
Building area: 817.51 sqm
Gross floor area ratio: 108.27%
Structure: reinforced concrete, steel frame
Finish: T24 pair glass, AL punched metal, exposed concrete

orim Publishing House, Paju. As well as
e main offices of Borim, a children's book
ıblisher, the building comprises a
arionette theatre

encouraged me to pursue the poetic influences of the place I came from and interpret them in spatial terms. So in my thesis I was actually looking at Chinese philosophy, the Yin and Yang, and Chi energy lines. It was a design process in which metaphor and reality came together and formed a physical entity. What remained of that period is an interest in architecture as a process rather than an object or a product.

How did you translate this poetic, subjective approach into a real-world design process when you opened your practice back in Seoul?

My early projects were deeply influenced by my years at Cooper, particularly the Museum of Shamanism. That was an excellent first project because even though I am Korean I knew very little about the culture of shamanism, that is a truly important part of spirituality and culture here. I did a lot of research into the way shamans used light and sound, and attempted to fold some of those aspects into the proposal. At the time it was perceived as an extremely radical design – I was introducing an approach to architecture that was totally alien to the Korean background at the time. I did unusual things like photograph the site with a kaleidoscope so that the topography was fractured arbitrarily, and then operated a translation into 3D by pushing and pulling the shards and figuring out ways to bring light into the space. It was a very meaningful project for me, but the unfortunate epilogue is that the client ran out of money and the museum was never built.

House of Open Books
Architects: Hailim Suh + Junsung Kim (Himma)
Location: Munbalri, Gyohaeup, Paju
Site area: 1,518.1 sqm
Gross floor area: 2,148.76 sqm
Building area: 727.21 sqm
Gross floor area ratio: 130.89%
Structure: reinforced concrete, steel frame
Finish: aluminium curtain wall, transparent and translucent glass, wood deck, exposed concrete

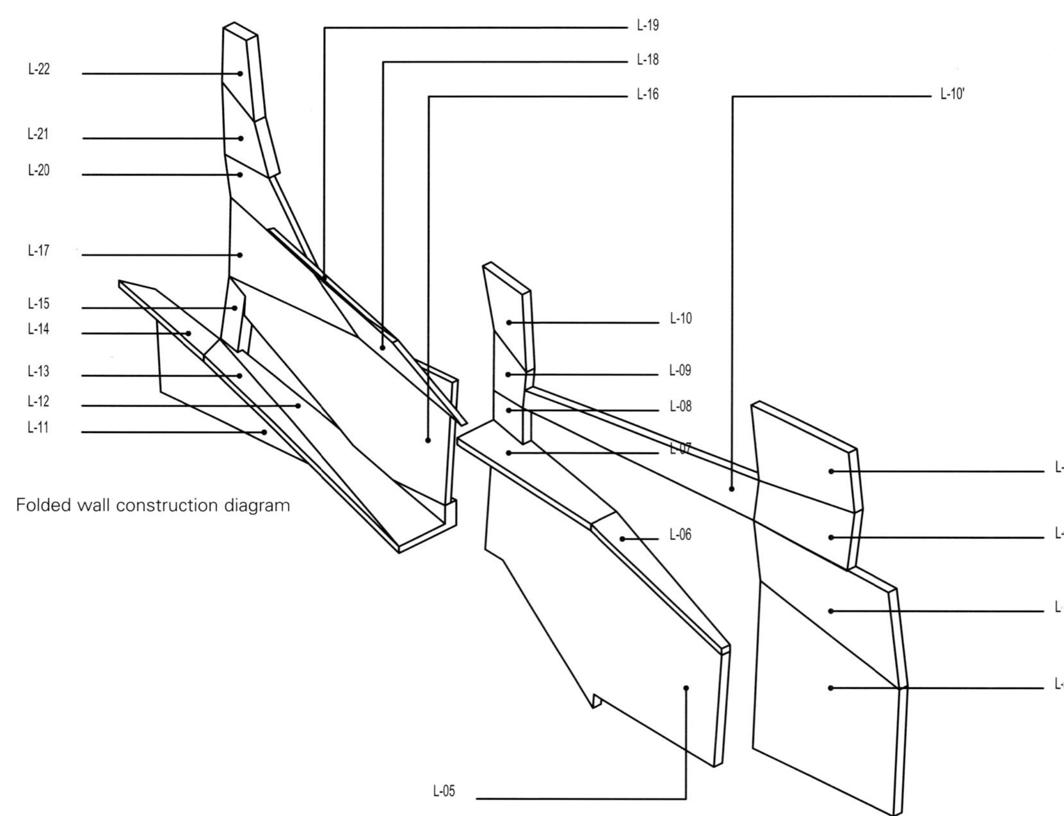

Folded wall construction diagram

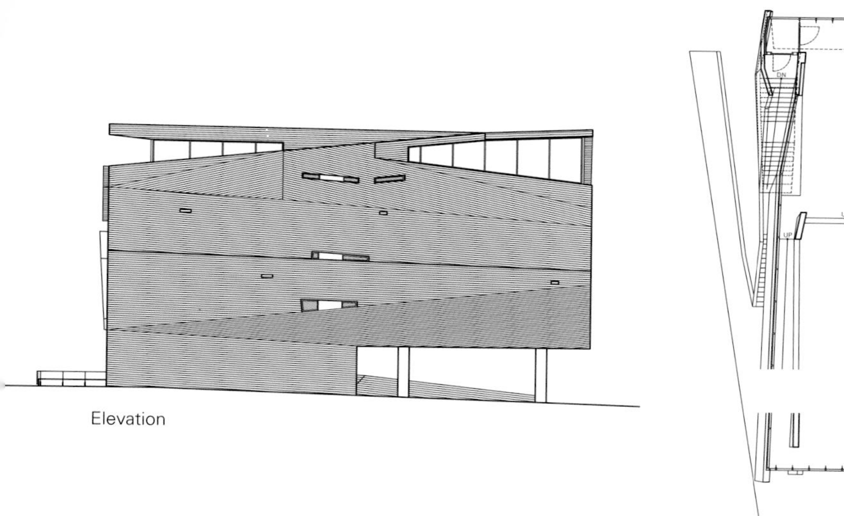

Elevation

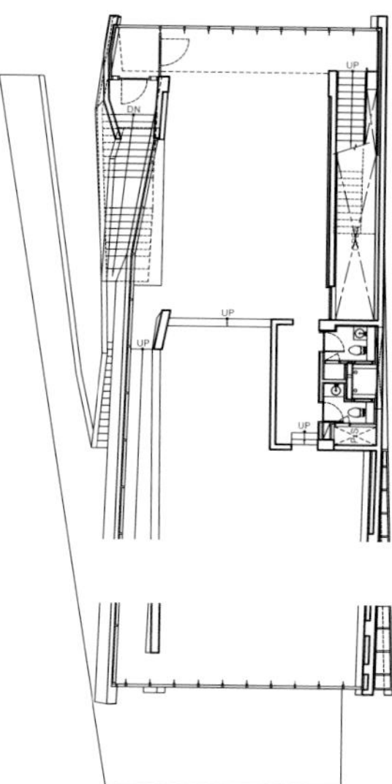

Third floor plan

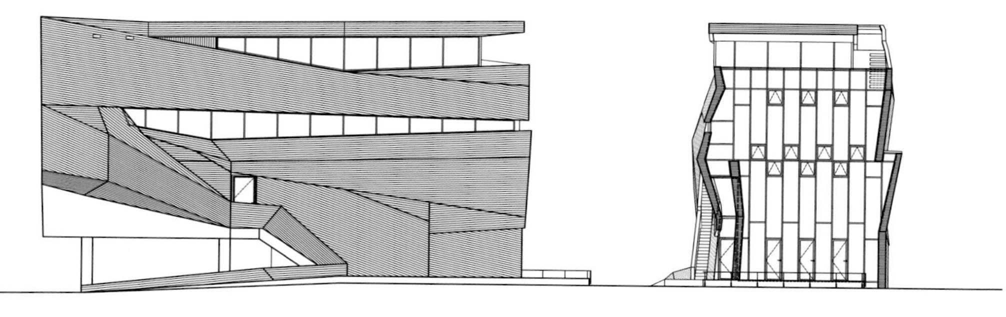

Elevation

Section

Opposite
House of Open Books, Paju

Following pages
Hangil Book Hall was designed in 2002 by SHoP Architects (New York) in conjunction with Himma & Junsung Kim. Located at the foot of one of the six hills that constitute the Heyri Art Valley district, the building is the main headquarters of Hangil Publishing, a well-known publisher of art and philosophy books in Korea

최진경 · 희로애락
HAS
BOOK HOUSE
3F
2F
GALLERY
1-2F
BOOKSHOP
ARTSHOP
1F
B1
GALLERY
CONCERT HALL

ouse C17, a private residence
the Heyri Art Valley

Kim Jong Kyu

Kim Jong Kyu (MARU, Seoul)

Your practice, MARU, was charged with designing the masterplan of Paju Book City, one of the most significant episodes in contemporary South Korean architecture. In many ways it was a turning point for your generation of designers in that it gave a large number of them the opportunity to cut their teeth on their first medium-size, non-residential design project, usually with a reasonable budget and a generous amount of creative freedom. Many of the works featured in this book, including your own Youl Hwa Dang Publishing House, are part of Paju Book City. Can you tell us about the genesis of the project and the thinking behind your masterplan?

The Book City is an industrial estate comprised of three hundred publishing and multimedia companies located in Paju, quite close to the DMZ area and the border with North Korea. It's the result of a process that started over a decade ago when Yi Ki-Ung, the chairman of South Korea's Publishers' Association, expressed the desire to find a single, centralised location where all the publishing companies could build their headquarters. When the scheme is complete, all of South Korea's publishing, binding, papermaking, design, printing and shipping will take place in Paju, making it one of the most important industrial centres in the country. An interesting feature of the site is that in the event of a future reunification of North and South Korea, Paju Book City would find itself on one of the main arteries connecting Seoul and Pyongyang.

My office worked closely on this project with ARU, a London-based practice led by Florian Beigel and Philip Christou. From the beginning we decided to avoid the word 'masterplan' – we prefer to describe our intervention as design guidelines, a sort of manual for how to build Paju. There was a strong desire both on our part and on the part of the Publishers' Association to make this an opportunity for expression for Korean architects. Our guidelines establish a general framework that regulates massing, typology of use and the relationship between individual buildings. It also deals with some contingent site-related issues.

Paju Book City is built on an elongated, three-kilometre-long plot sandwiched between a mountain and a highway embankment, beyond which River Han lies. Much of the site is a marshland, and there are considerable drainage issues. Rather than elevating the entire site and dealing with the hydrological problems underground, we decided to preserve some of the marshes, creating what we call an 'urban wetland' – a topography of elevated building plots intersected by wetland corridors and streams. Our guidelines set the construction parameters both in plan and in section. In section, an important datum is given by the height of the highway embankment, which is the height limit for the factories lined up along it. The backbone of Paju Book City is Bookmakers Street, which is lined on both sides by publishing houses. These are shuffled in plan so they don't block each other's views towards the river and the mountain.

Paju has also given a number of international practices their first opportunity to build in Korea. What was the intention in inviting firms such as Foreign Office Architects to build here?

Xaveer de Geyter, Kazuyo Sejima and Stan Allen all have projects here too. Inviting them was a way of raising the bar a bit while reinforcing Paju's role as an epicentre in Korea for contemporary architecture, and was also a way of enhancing the development's visibility on an international level.

Your own practice, MARU, designed one of the first publishing houses to actually be built. Was it intended to act as an example of how your design guidelines might be interpreted?

Yes, to some extent it was. Youl Hwa Dang building was commissioned by the chairman of the Publishers' Association himself, so it also had to express his vision for the future of Paju. This design too was carried out together with ARU (Florian Beigel). The building folds a number of different programmes into a single volume. The lower part of the building is occupied by two-floor studio residences for some of the staff and writers in residence, and a pavilion on the top floor houses the publishing offices. This complies with our prescription that only rooftop pavilions should rise above the datum given by the highway embankment so as to preserve the views from the various offices across Paju.

MARU also produced the design guidelines for Heyri Art Valley, another new urban complex not far from Paju Book City. Are the two developments connected in any way?

Heyri is a slightly different story. First of all, the publishers and staff working in Paju needed somewhere to live. Since Paju is zoned for industrial and not residential use, we couldn't build very many dwellings there. So a number of partners in the Publishers' As-

Paju Book City
Architects: Seung Hchioh Sang, co-ordinator; Florian Beigel, Kim Jong Kyu, Kim Young Joon, Min Hyun Sik

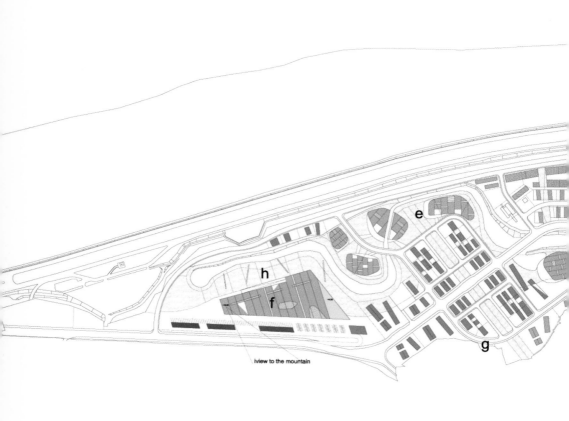

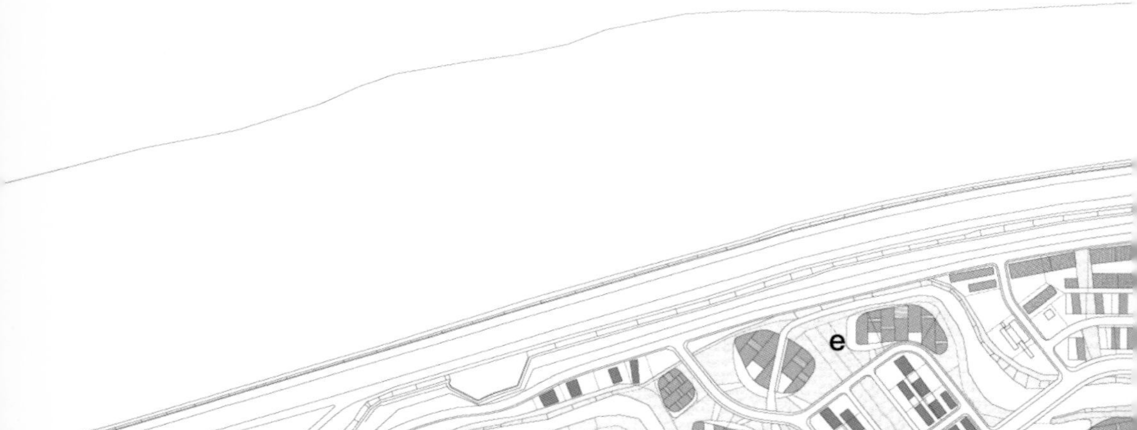

Site plan

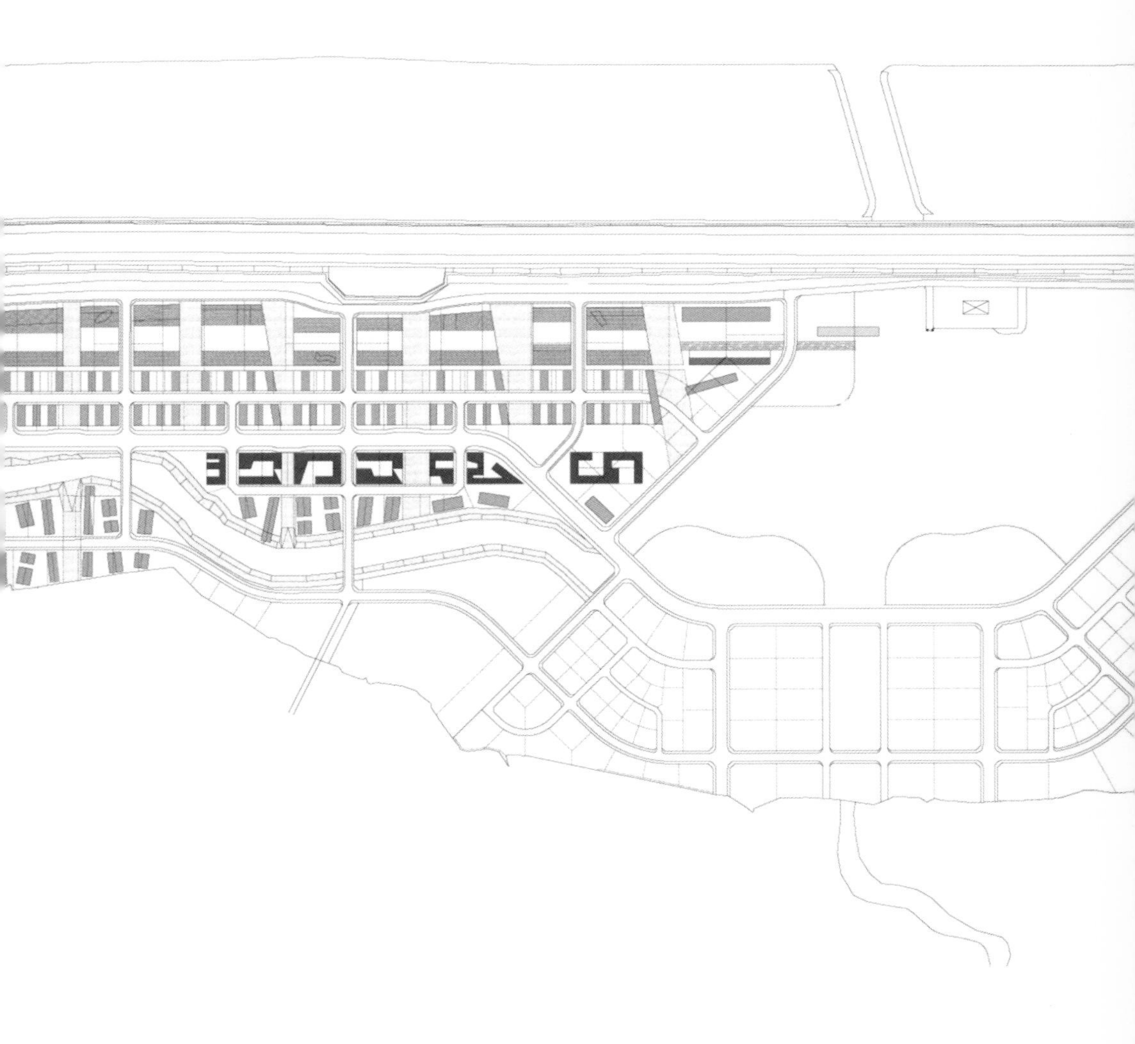

sociation bought plots of land in a nearby valley called Heyri with the intention of developing it into a residential and cultural equivalent of Paju. We were commissioned to produce a 'design manual' for the area, and that's how Heyri Art Valley was born. Over time, the valley has attracted a number of artists, performers and other people involved in creative professions, and that in turn has attracted several galleries and museums. As with Paju, many of the galleries and houses in Heyri were designed by relatively young Korean architecture practices. I too designed several buildings in Heyri, but I consider the overall design guidelines to be a much greater accomplishment than the single buildings we conceived. The real challenge was giving character to a town that previously didn't exist.

Both Heyri and Paju strike me as having vaguely utopian undertones – a kind of escape-valve for the pent-up energies of a generation eager to build.

In some ways they are utopian projects. They are certainly very different from anything else in South Korea. To take a positive view of the phenomenon, I do believe they mark a turning point in the Korean public's recognition and understanding of contemporary architecture. Until now, buildings were evaluated in economic terms only, but I think today there is a lot more appreciation of the work of architects and the added value of design.

Like many of the most successful Korean architects of your generation, you studied abroad – at the Architectural Association in London, in your case – and then returned to Seoul. How has this process of cultural infiltration influenced contemporary Korean architecture? I this an ongoing phenomenon?

It is ongoing – even today, many young Koreans tra el to Europe or the US to study. But it's changing. Th quality of university education in South Korea has im proved dramatically in the past twenty years, and a larg number of our courses are now internationally certifie and recognised by foreign professional bodies like R BA. I think the question of how this has influenced ou architectural culture is quite a subjective issue. Person ally, I am often told by my Western associates, like Flo rian, that my design process remains deeply Oriental de spite my years abroad.

What relationship, if any, exists between Korean an Japanese architects at this moment?

Despite the physical proximity, there isn't much com munication. Japanese architecture enjoys a lot more in ternational recognition than ours, but it's an interestin model for us to observe. I think Korea is at the beginnin of a phase that Japan is already well into, but there ar still substantial differences. There's very little govern ment support for architecture here, for example. In Japa the government is much more supportive, and high-qua ity contemporary architecture is recognised as an im portant part of the national identity. In a way there ar more points of contact with some of the other South Western Asian countries, such as Indonesia or the Philip pines. There are numerous interesting similarities wit these countries, especially in terms of urban developmen in relation to a sudden influx of substantial wealth an capital. It's a phenomenon we are carrying out some re search projects on at the moment.

Editorial offices of Youl Hwa Dang Publishing in Paju Book City.
Kim Jong Kyu & MARU, together with Florian Beigel & ARU, drew up the design guidelines for Paju Book City. Youl Hwa Dang Publishing House, one of the first buildings to be built on the site, was intended as an example of a possible interpretation of these design guidelines. The sloping glass panes of the translucent windows increase in height towards the top of the building to compensate for the effects of perspective

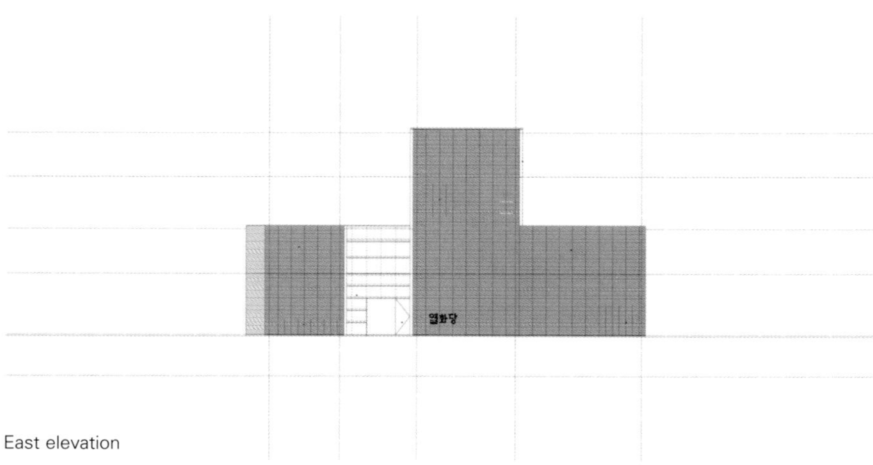

East elevation

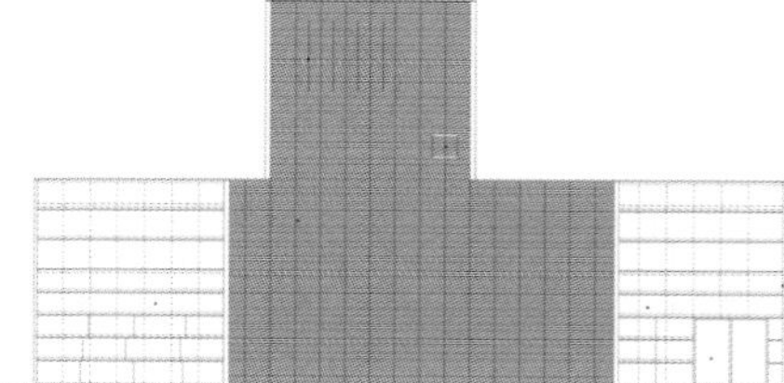

West elevation

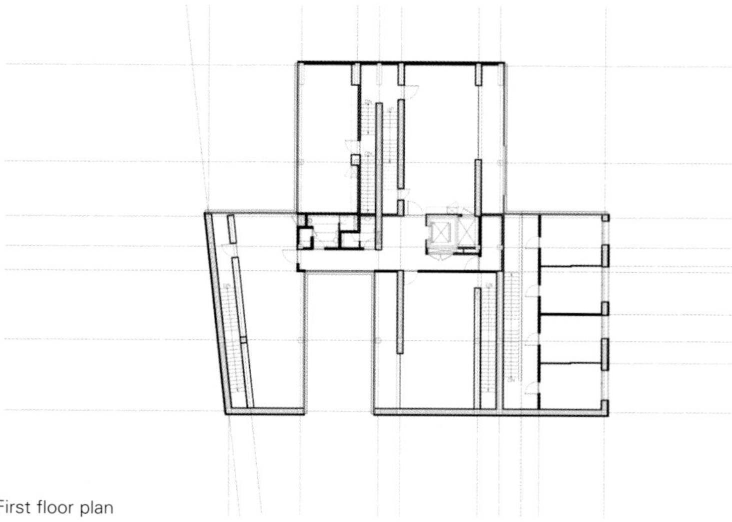

First floor plan

ul Hwa Dang Publishing House
chitects: Kim Jong Kyu,
etropolitan Architecture
esearch Unit, Seoul
ang Kyoung Hwa, Choi Jong
un); Florian Beigel, Architecture
esearch Unit, London
hilip Christou, Bae Sang Sou,
in Jun Kee)
ontractor: Dong
yuk Construction
ructural engineer: Seoul
ructural Engineering
te area: 1,758 sqm
tal floor area: 1,683 sqm

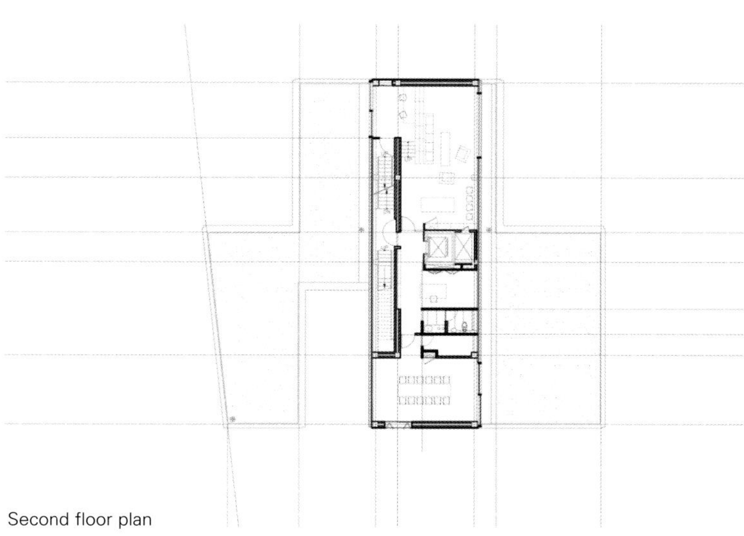
Second floor plan

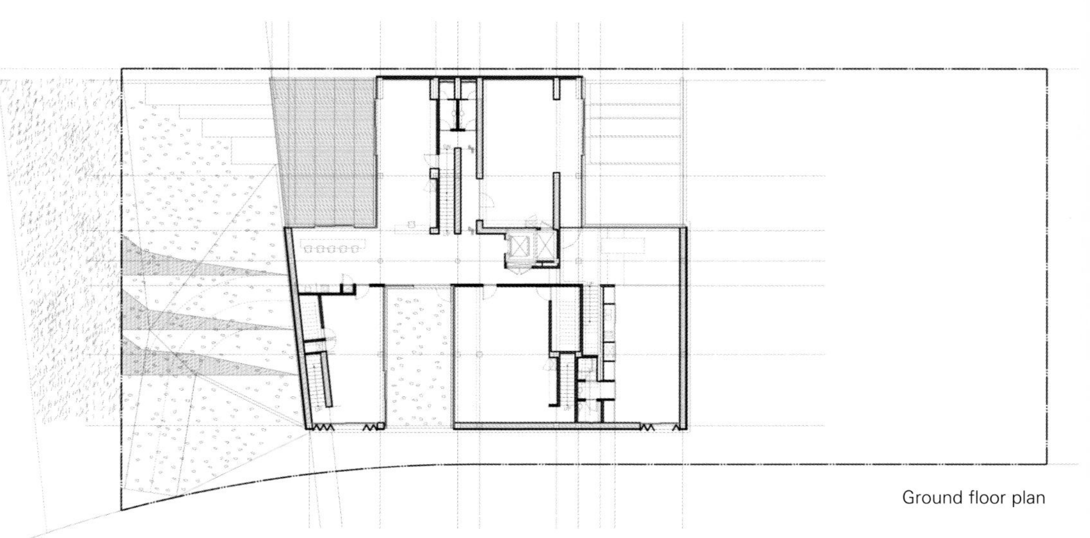
Ground floor plan

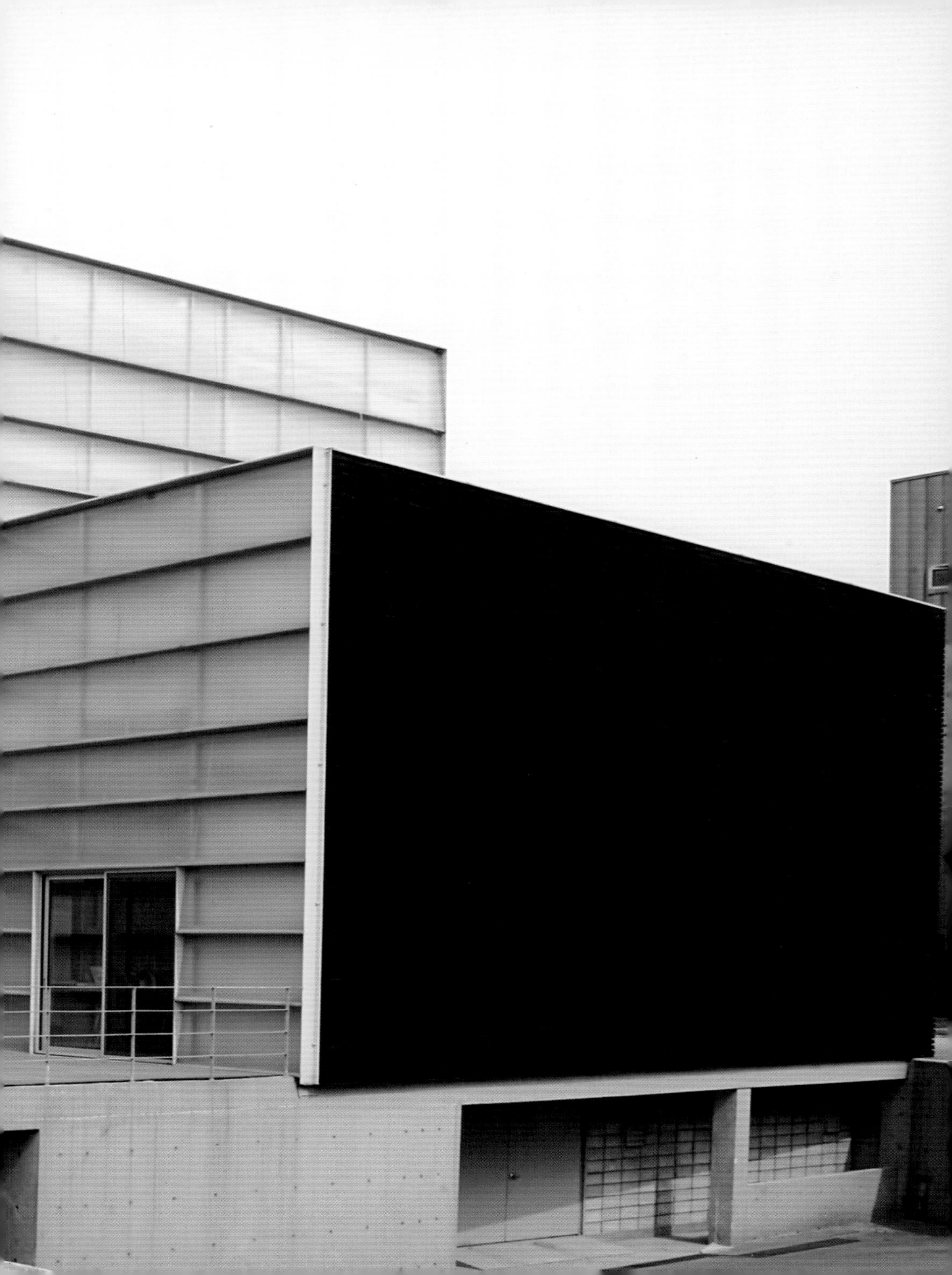

House Equals City
A Conversation with Taro Igarashi

First of all, I'd like to ask you about the relationship between contemporary architecture and the distinctive qualities that typify Tokyo's urban fabric. Looking at recent architecture in Tokyo, and in particular projects such as the Moriyama houses or works by Atelier Bow-Wow, one gets the impression that the younger generation is more sensitive, or one might even say protective, towards the diminutive scale of intervention that characterises traditional urbanism. Do you think this is the case?

It is, to various degrees according to the various practices. The most obvious example of this is to be found in Bow-Wow's publications *Pet Architecture* and *Made in Tokyo*. Their observations propose a completely new model for engaging the city. But one thing that is worth pointing out is that there are many different ways to engage the existing context – for example, it can be just as much about the voids as the solids. Nishizawa's Moriyama houses subtly reference the traditional Japanese *roji*, or the gaps between the buildings, in the arrangements of the masses on the site. *Roji* are the microscopic alleyways that run between the buildings in the oldest areas of the city such as the wooden-building districts near Ueno Park. *Roji*-type streets aren't necessarily unique to Tokyo, but it's difficult to think of anywhere that they have survived and remained an integral part of a city's urbanism – even for newly built buildings – until this day. After WW2 in Tokyo a huge amount of reconstruction work was needed, and an area almost the size of New York City was rebuilt. Pressing need for both infrastructure and shelter meant that the city planners did not have the time to integrally implement their ideas for a truly modern city, so they focused on infrastructure redevelopment with the objective of relaunching the economy, while residential reconstruction was left to local authorities. For this reason, the prewar layout served as the basis for reconstruction with the consequence that alleyway-type housing that had evolved from village habitats remained the dominant typology in many areas.

Roji type was occasionally evoked by the Modernist architects of the postwar decades, although the scale of their interventions was completely different. Fumihiko Maki's Hillside Terrace in Daikanyama, which was developed over a period of thirty years from the 1960s through to the 1990s, is a very large-scale intervention that succeeds in evoking the atmosphere of the *roji* in the spaces between the buildings. The analogies between the Moriyama houses and the micro-urbanism of the *roji* alleyways is much more explicit, in that it reproposes the poetry of the fragmentary fabric that still today dominates much of Tokyo's cityscape. There are many subtle nods to traditional Japanese domestic architecture in that complex. For example, to access his bathroom, Moriyama-san must step outside his house and enter a separate cubicle. This is reminiscent of the *sento*, or communal bathhouses that were common in Japanese cities until the post-war boom when for the first time each family could afford to have its own facilities.

One of the distinctive features of Tokyo, still the largest city in the world today, is the tightly-packed ocean of single-family houses that make up the vast majority of its suburban fabric. What led to the institution of the one-building-per-plot rule?

Traditionally, there were practical reasons to not have large buildings and to keep each dwelling disconnected from all the others. Tokyo's residential neighbourhoods were largely constructed out of wood, and even a modest earthquake could set off fires that would certainly wreak havoc through vast tracts of the suburban districts. Separating buildings increased the chances of being able to control fires, and this led to the distinctive cityscapes you still see today, in which it is almost impossible to find a continuous wall connecting houses. A series of other measures were also taken to limit the possible damage from fires – these neighbourhoods of micro-dwellings are occasionally dissected by larger streets lined by commercial buildings on either side to a depth of 30 metres. These streets effectively act as fire-breakers, surrounding the low-rise residential areas and heightening the village-like atmosphere that permeates them. In recent years, there has been an increasing tendency for high-rise developments to encroach on these low-rise neighbourhoods, and other anti-earthquake measures such as the widening of streets to allow access for emergency vehicles are slowly eroding the alleyway urbanism of some neighbourhoods.

Speaking of large-scale complexes, Yoshiharu Tsukamoto points out the correlation between the size of buildings and the size of the commercial enterprises that operate in them. The small family-run shops, restaurants and crafts-people's workshops you still see in abundance in the 'suburban villages' that make up so much of Tokyo are excluded a priori from the new large-scale commercial development springing up around Tokyo. According to him this is the reason why these complexes are so often soulless and 'dead'. Are these family-run micro-entities destined to disappear under the pressure of chain stores and retail malls? What effect could it have on the city's urban fabric?

When the Omotesando Hills complex by Tadao Ando opened there was a huge outcry for precisely this reason. It was a symbol of the large versus small. When it opened in 2005, it created much controversy as its construction involved the demolishing of the Dojunkai Aoyama Apartments, originally constructed in 1927 as the first public reinforced-concrete apartments in Japan. To keep consistent with the trees that line Omotesando Avenue, it doesn't go above six stories, but in addition to that it goes six stories below ground level. The whole Omotesando Hills complex houses over 130 shops and 38 apartments, and an almost unique feature of this complex is that it's fronted by a continuous, uninterrupted wall almost 250 metres long. The interesting thing is that it took

Mori, the construction company and developer, twenty years to buy up all the individual apartment plots necessary to realise that one project. It's amazing if you think about the unbelievable difference between Japan and China in this sense – in Beijing, a project like that could be easily realised in one year. It highlights the huge difference that can be made to the way a city works by legislation on matters such as eminent domain. In Japan the regulations are such that Mori had to negotiate with each landowner for each subdivision. For this reason, it's not as simple as one might imagine to build large-scale complexes like Omotesando Hills. The further you go into the residential neighbourhoods, the more fragmented the plots become, and the more complicated it becomes to put together a large plot. Of course it is happening anyway, but it's a lot more gradual here than it might be elsewhere.

Are there any other invisible forces at play on Tokyo's urban landscape?

There are some legislative idiosyncrasies in Japan that have, over the years, exerted an involuntary but powerful influence on the city's residential neighbourhoods. The inheritance taxes here are exorbitantly high, and this has progressively led to a rather troubling hyper-subdivision of building plots. The heirs who inherit a lot from a relative have to pay a tax so high that they are almost invariably obliged to sell a portion of their lot so as to be able to pay the tax, and the outcome is a stock of excessively small houses, very little green space and a substantial number of rather absurdly-shaped plots.

In general, do you think the younger generation of Japanese architects is at all interested in finding a key entry-point to engage tradition in the way you suggested Nishizawa's Moriyama houses do?

I actually think that younger Japanese architects have very little conscious interest in investigating architecture from the past, distant or recent. But I get the distinct impression there is a strong desire to push the conventions of urban living to the very limits. The situation in the city has completely changed in the last ten or fifteen years, and on many different levels. To give you one example: there are now so many *kombini* (convenience stores) in Tokyo that almost everyone will have one at less than a minute's walk from where they live. Surprisingly, this has a very tangible effect on architecture, in that it means that people can live in much smaller spaces. Many people actually live without a fridge and by doing only very minimal cooking.

It's a challenge, but it's possible, and if it means you can get a smaller space in a better neighbourhood, a lot of people think it's worth it. I actually experimented with this myself – I tried living without a fridge for a year. As a result, architects have more flexibility in designing dwellings, since many of the practical issues that involve equipment and preparation space can be simply eliminated. Another thing is that cities in Japan are actually very safe, so people feel less of a need to fortify their dwellings against outsiders. What the ubiquitous *kombini* did for covenience, the *koban* (police box) did for safety.

Do you think these changes in social customs will mean we will be seeing more rather Spartan housing projects similar to the one commissioned by Mr Moriyama?

The Moriyama houses are still a very special case. Living there is a real lifestyle choice – it's not a typical situation. The architecture imposes a very particular lifestyle on you, and some people would probably never get used to that degree of exposure or of minimalism.

Looking at the work of Japanese architects today, it can be quite difficult to trace a direct line of thought or influence connecting them to the work of the Metabolists and the heroic years of the post-war era. As Tsukamoto points out, though, the influence of some of their contemporaries, such as Shinohara, is much more evident.

I don't think it's so much a case of individual influences as a shift in the condition of the city. The Metabolists were operating in a very particular environment, and at a very particular time, and those times have now changed. In the 1950s and 1960s there was an idea of the house as a fortress, something designed to fight (or at least resist) the city, such as Kikutake's Sky House. Another example is the Tower House by Takamitsu Azuma, finished in 1967, which has a fortress-like appearance. But for the generation of Bow-Wow, those working today, the house merges into the city. They don't think house *versus* city but house *equals* city. The way of thinking about the city has changed radically, and architecture has changed with it. Having said that, I think the work of Toyo Ito does bridge the generations. In 1980, he changed his style radically. Before then his architecture tended to be closed and introverted, but in the 1980s his work became much lighter and turned around to embrace its environment. In a way you could describe him as a meeting point for the two generations. Another important turning point for Japanese cities, and consequently for architects, was the period of the bubble economy in the 1980s. There was a lot of money, and for the first time people started to really *enjoy* city life. The *kombini* appeared, and people went out and had fun. Japan's powerhouse years, until 1989, were a period of phenomenal growth – over 5% a year. For a while, the real estate market in Tokyo was the hottest in the world. It somehow made people forget about fortifying their architecture and signalled the turn towards a search for purity and ephemerality in architecture.

Given that squares and large open spaces are relatively uncommon in Tokyo, what would you describe as the prevailing typology of 'public space'?

The square or the piazza is a device for mingling, and you can probably say the same about the *roji*, in a slightly different way. I think these small streets and alleyways are the place where encounters and exchanges occur. But on the whole there isn't that much public space in Japanese cities – capitalism has prevailed over public space. And what little public space there is doesn't function particularly well. There used to be a lot more mobile micro-commerce than there is today – food carts, restaurant wagons on wheels and so on – and they encouraged a more 'domestic' use of the street. They're still relatively common in China and Korea, but have almost completely disappeared here. Atelier Bow-Wow recently did a project in which they rebuilt one of these 'restaurants on wheels' – it's called White Limousine Yatai. It is part of an experiment of gathering space in the city by introducing small mobile structures, a form of urban furniture, to create one's own 'Micro Public Space'. It's a way of taking even the tiniest space that is officially 'public' but adding a personal layer to it and making use of this space.

Taro Igarashi is architectural critic and professor at Tohoku University. Born in 1967 in Paris, he lives and works in Tokyo. Doctor of Engineering from Tokyo University. Currently associate professor at Tohoku University and adjunct professor at Tokyo National University of Fine Arts and Music, and Yokohama National University. His numerous publications include *Owari no Kenchiku / Hajimari no Kenchiku* (Architecture of the End / Architecture of the Beginning), *Shin-shukyo to Kyodai-kenchiku* (New Religions and Gigantic Architecture), *Senso to Kenchiku* (War and Architecture) and *Kaboubi Toshi* (City of Excessive Defence). He has also co-authored *Birudingutaipu no Kaibogaku* (Anatomy of Building Types) with Okawa Nobuyuki.

JAPAN

Masaki Endoh with his daughter

lasaki Endoh (EDH, Tokyo)

'atural Ellipse, the house you designed for a private 'ient in the Shibuya neighbourhood, is one of the most nusual responses we have seen to the hyper-density f contemporary Tokyo. Could you tell us about this roject?

Natural Ellipse is probably the most interesting uilding I have worked on to date, and I think that's the esult of the very particular circumstances that surounded its inception. I love sports, so I like to use the ietaphor of a football match to explain this project. A ood match is defined by uncertainty as to who will win. ne teams are well balanced, unexpected situations ise, and there are lots of supporters looking on: in such situation the winning goal will be truly memorable beause it stirs the emotions of the spectators. It was exctly the same for Natural Ellipse. There were so many onstraints imposed on the design that it required a uge amount of creative perseverance to come up with solution, and until the end it was uncertain if we ould succeed. Ultimately, the result was far more ineresting than if we had been working with a more onventional brief. The site is extremely central, just a ew minutes walk from Shibuya station. The client nose this location for its convenience – people who ork in the area often commute two or three hours to et to their offices, whereas he could walk. But there ere major drawbacks too: first of all, this is the 'love otel' district – it's where couples come for privacy if ieir flats are too small and they want to get away om their families. In this context, the client didn't ant to have any windows looking out onto the street, hich resulted in a very introverted building. Second, ne value of land is very high in this area, so the plot is inuscule in size, which made it was very difficult to t two apartments onto the site.

Why two apartments?

A common strategy for tackling the unbelievably igh cost of land here in Tokyo is to build not one but wo apartments on these tiny plots. Building a house om scratch requires major capital investment, so lients usually have to borrow large sums from the ank. To be able to pay back the mortgage, they build separate mini-apartment into their house and rent it ut to a tenant. This means that the conditions are very ramped for a number of years, but when they have nished paying back the mortgage they can join the two partments and gain an extra bedroom, perhaps for one of their children. It's a very interesting strategy – more and more people are becoming 'micro-developers' to deal with the exorbitant price of land and real estate.

How is the space inside divided up between the two apartments?

The owner has the basement and the third and fourth floors, and the tenant lives in the first and second floors. A spiral staircase runs through the core and connects the owner's basement study to the upper floors. Since we couldn't place any windows on the outer shell for reasons of privacy, the best solution would have been to have some kind of a courtyard. And since the site was too small for that we had to settle for a well that brings light into the upper apartment. I'm very interested in prefabrication, so the original intention was to make the shell out of prefabricated fibreglass panels assembled on site, but unfortunately this was not possible because no two panels were the same shape and the fabrication process would have been hugely expensive. So we eventually decided to clad a steel skeleton in fibre-reinforced plastic (FRP), although to do this we had to solve some fire safety issues by treating the materials with a special coating. This skeleton is comprised of twenty-four vertical elliptical rings that form an oval. Through the modification of the base and height ratios, these elliptical rings define the building's interior spaces.

The real value of property in Tokyo is often the land it is built on, whereas buildings themselves often have relatively short life spans. It's not uncommon for a house to be purchased only to be demolished and rebuilt. As an architect, what is your attitude towards this? Do you worry that your buildings might meet such a fate?

On the whole I'm in favour of this situation. I've always been a great admirer of Buckminster Fuller, and he was a great advocate of short-life-span buildings. My only concern in this regard is sustainability, but I think that we use less materials than other countries precisely because the intended life span is shorter, so the situation ultimately evens out. It makes particular sense in Japan because we have such an unusual urban fabric made up of small plots and leftover spaces. In any case, I don't think it's worth trying to change this situation – it might actually be more efficient this way.

Natural Ellipse
Architects: Endoh Design House & MIAS
Location: Shibuya shopping district, Tokyo
Site area: 52.99 sqm
Building area: 31.20 sqm
Total floor area: 131.74 sqm
Structure: steel

Most of the work you have shown us is residential architecture. Do you plan to diversify the activity of your practice in the future?

I've recently received some larger commissions, but it took me some time to secure projects beyond the scale of the individual dwelling. I think it's an issue that faces many architects of our generation. There are similarities with the situation in certain European countries. I've heard people complain there is an entire generation having difficulties going beyond restorations and conversions, and here we have the same problem getting beyond the stage of commissions for small houses. Part of the problem is that in Japan the big construction companies carve out territories for themselves, and it's very hard to break into their markets. Anybody can list the names of the big construction companies, but very few people could tell you the names of more than two or three architects.

Takaharu Tezuka, one of the other architects interviewed for this book, complained that he frequently sees his kindergarten project published with no reference to himself, although the name of the construction company is often listed.

Traditionally, especially in our small towns, houses were designed and built by skilled carpenters. Today that is not the case, of course, but many people see the contemporary equivalent of the carpenter in the contractor. If they need a house, their first port of call is a large construction company. It must be said, though, that something is changing in this respect. The younger generation, especially in Tokyo and other large cities is increasingly likely to commission an architect to produce a design for their specific site.

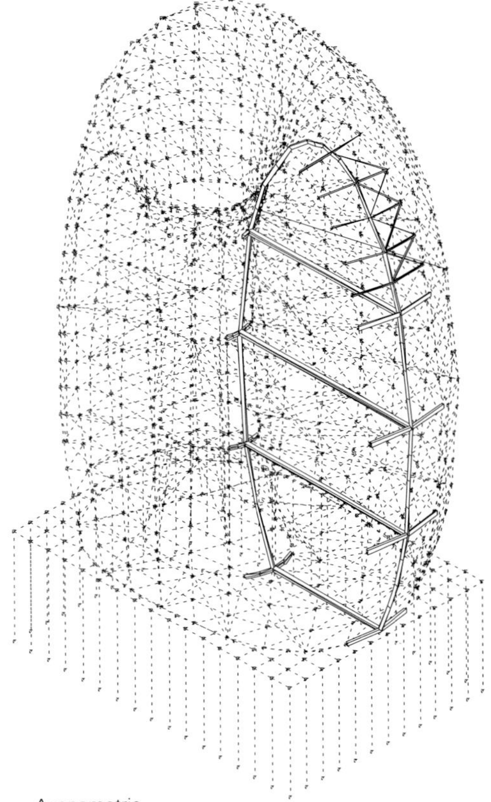

Axonometric

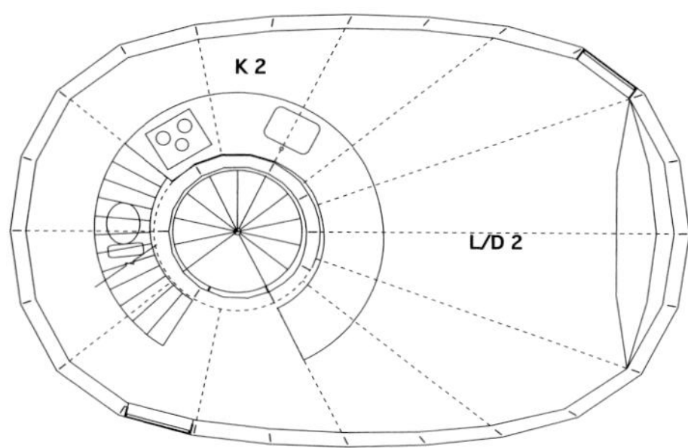

Third floor

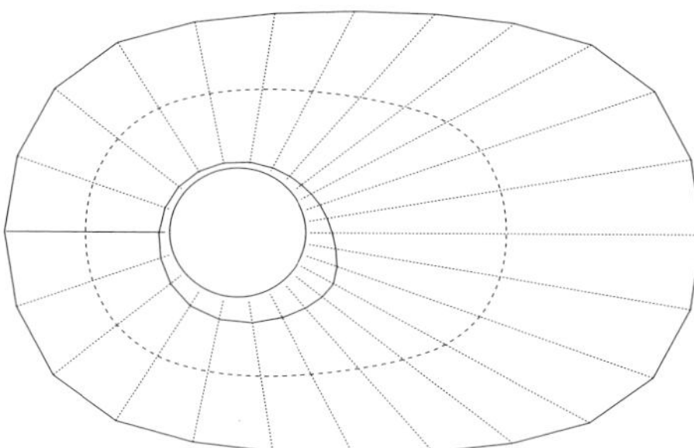

Roof

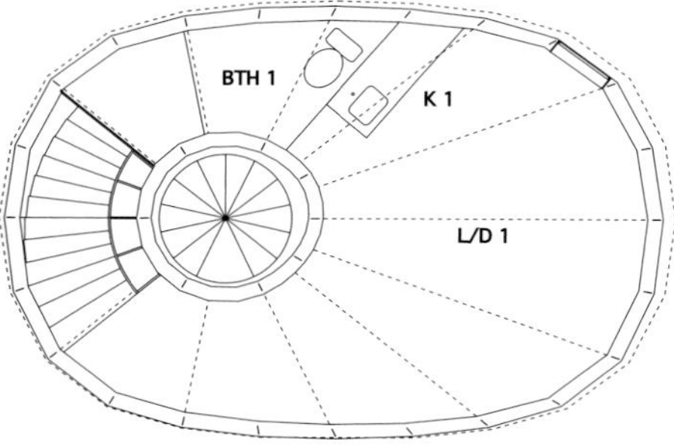

Second floor

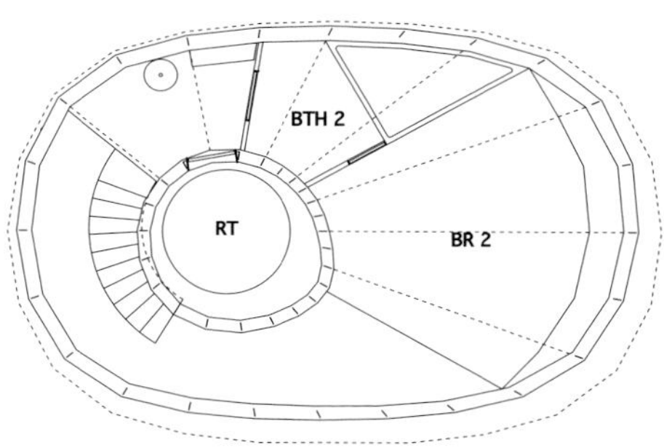

Fourth floor

Previous pages and opposite
Natural Ellipse is situated in the vicinity of Shibuya station, Tokyo, in a neighbourhood occupied primarily by short-stay hotels. The building is particularly introverted, drawing most of its light from a central light well, with almost no openings onto the adjacent streets. The building's shell is constituted of FRP, or polymer resin poured over fibreglass, a lightweight and relatively strong material that is versatile and economical enough to permit the realisation of Endoh's atypical solution to the site's distinctly exposed position

ホワイトBOX

Junya Ishigami

unya Ishigami (Tokyo)

fter working for Kazuyo Sejima's office for five years, ɔu started up your own practice with a design for a ɣper-thin table that elevates a common item of furni-ʳre to a condition of diagrammatic purity. As with much ᶠ Sejima's own work, the table's apparent simplicity the result of a complex feat of engineering. Could you ll us a bit about this design?

The table was an experiment – a way of explor-g the possibilities of design through removal of mass ıd substance. I designed two versions of this table: e first was approximately 4 metres long, but the eel tabletop spanning these 4 metres was only 3 mm ick. Although it was a perfectly normal table in every :her sense, this hyper-thinness gave it a surreal, al-ost unnatural appearance. In reality it could actual-be used to support objects. I decided to push the ɔncept even further, and produced a second version hich was 10 metres long by 2.5 metres wide, and ıll only 3 mm thick. Although it couldn't be used for ʳactical purposes – the surface ripples if you touch – there is something almost magical about it... I ɔnsider it more an installation artwork than a piece ᶠ furniture. It was exhibited at Miami Basel art fair a ɔuple of years ago.

How did you achieve this extraordinary thinness?

In both tables, a lot of work went into under-:anding how to pre-stress the steel tabletops. I orked with a structural engineer to carry out the cal-ılations. They had to be manufactured with exactly e right amount of curvature so that they would raighten out under their own weight and appear per-ctly flat. The tabletop is essentially a giant leaf-spring if you rest it on its side it springs into a teardrop ıape. That's how we shipped it to the museum in rael that purchased it.

There is a remarkable consistency between the nguage you use in your architecture, in your industrial esign and in projects such as the table that you de-ıe as artworks or installations. Do you really see them ɜ separate disciplines?

I see architecture as a subset of art, so for me ere's no specific boundary between them. 'Industri-design' is actually more a description of the way something is manufactured than what it is: I often use furniture as a form of 'interior architecture', as a way of making spaces human and inhabitable.

Your first architecture project is nearing comple-tion now...

Yes. While I was still working for Sejima, I was com-missioned to design a new technical facility for the Kana-gawa Institute of Technology. It was a great opportuni-ty to set up my own practice. The programme of the build-ing is essentially a 2,000 square-metre workshop for stu-dents. I decided to build a giant shed with glass walls and a very thin roof supported by three hundred pillars. Seen in plan, the pillars appear to be scattered across the space completely randomly, but that's actually not the case. Deciding the layout of the pillars was one of the most complex aspects of the project.

For what reason?

First of all, because of structural issues. There are no cross-braces to stabilise the roof against horizontal forces such as the wind, so the pillars have the func-tion not only of supporting the roof but also of provid-ing lateral stabilisation. The glass on the exterior is sim-ply a curtain wall with no structural purpose. The pil-lars are all flat steel sheets, so their orientation be-comes very important in structural terms. Secondly, my intention was to use an increased density of pillars to create a sense of privacy and intimacy in this giant room. That's why establishing the distribution of the pil-lars also became a programmatic issue. Areas such as the workshop spaces and teaching spaces have much fewer pillars than the offices and the resting area. I've also been commissioned to design the furniture, so I intend to use this as an opportunity to experiment with the idea of considering the furniture as an architectur-al element in itself, a way of organising the space.

So there are no walls?

Exactly – that was the intention. If there are more pillars, less people will be able to occupy a given space and therefore it'll be more quiet, and vice-versa. One of the intentions was to make a building that seen in plan has some of the beauty of a star-chart. Just as there is variety in the density of constellations, and in

Kanagawa Institute of Technology
Architects: Junya Ishigami + Associates
Location: Atsugi, Kanagawa Prefecture
Structural engineers: Konishi Structural Engineers
Contractors: Kajima Corporation

Site area: 129,335 sqm
Building area: 1,989.15 sqm
Total floor area: 1,989.15 sqm
Structure: steel frame
Maximum height: 5,050 mm

the brightness of stars, here there are pillars of various depths and areas of different density.

It was extremely difficult to find the right kind of software to calculate all the possible permutations in the layout of the pillars. On the one hand there was the complexity of the structural system, and on the other we wanted to experience the sense of enclosure or openness that one would feel in different areas of the building. CAD software didn't really work for this, so we ended up developing a dedicated application specifically to help us optimise the layout of the pillars. Once you establish the density you want to achieve in different parts of the building, the software calculates the optimum distribution and orientation, saving us a lot of time. Since it was hard to imagine what the physical experience of the building would be like by just looking at a plan, we also started building lots of models.

From the models it looks as though the roof will be remarkably thin – in proportion, almost as thin as the tabletop.

The roof will be just 200 mm thick – to keep it that thin we had to set all the services into he floor plate.

Do you have any other architecture projects at the moment?

I'm currently working on a house for a single person, a young individual who commissioned me to de-sign a weekend retreat. The site is a relatively large plo in a suburb of Tokyo. I decided to develop it vertical – we will plant lots of very tall, slender trees across th site and around the house.

The idea is to create a totally transparent living spac that finds a form of privacy by being elevated above a the surrounding houses and partially concealed by tree I took a walk in a forest to select the type I wanted t plant on the site. The bedroom will reach a height of a most 10 metres, and to accentuate the sense of im materiality of the architecture we will use acrylic wall which are very expensive but even more transparen than glass. When you are in the bedroom you will be ab to see the trees swaying just outside. The ground floo is enclosed, but there is no floor, just raw earth – a so of enclosed garden. The bathroom is set below grade There is only one staircase, which is external and has structural purpose in reinforcing the house's extreme thin steel frame. The challenge was to make the spac thermally comfortable. The trees will cast some shad on the bedroom in the summer, and there will be cu tains to keep the sun out. The roof and floor are coate with a special high-efficiency insulation. You can't real call this project a house in the conventional sense of th word – it's more like a 'habitable space' in a forest, some thing closer to a treehouse than a house.

Opposite
A forest of apparently randomly placed structural pillars constitutes the structural system of Ishigami's extension to the Kanagawa Institute of Technology

pp. 192–93
Iterations of the possible arrangements of the pillars that support the building's ceiling. These vertical members are arranged so as to create areas of privacy, where they are more dense, and a sense of openness where they are less dense

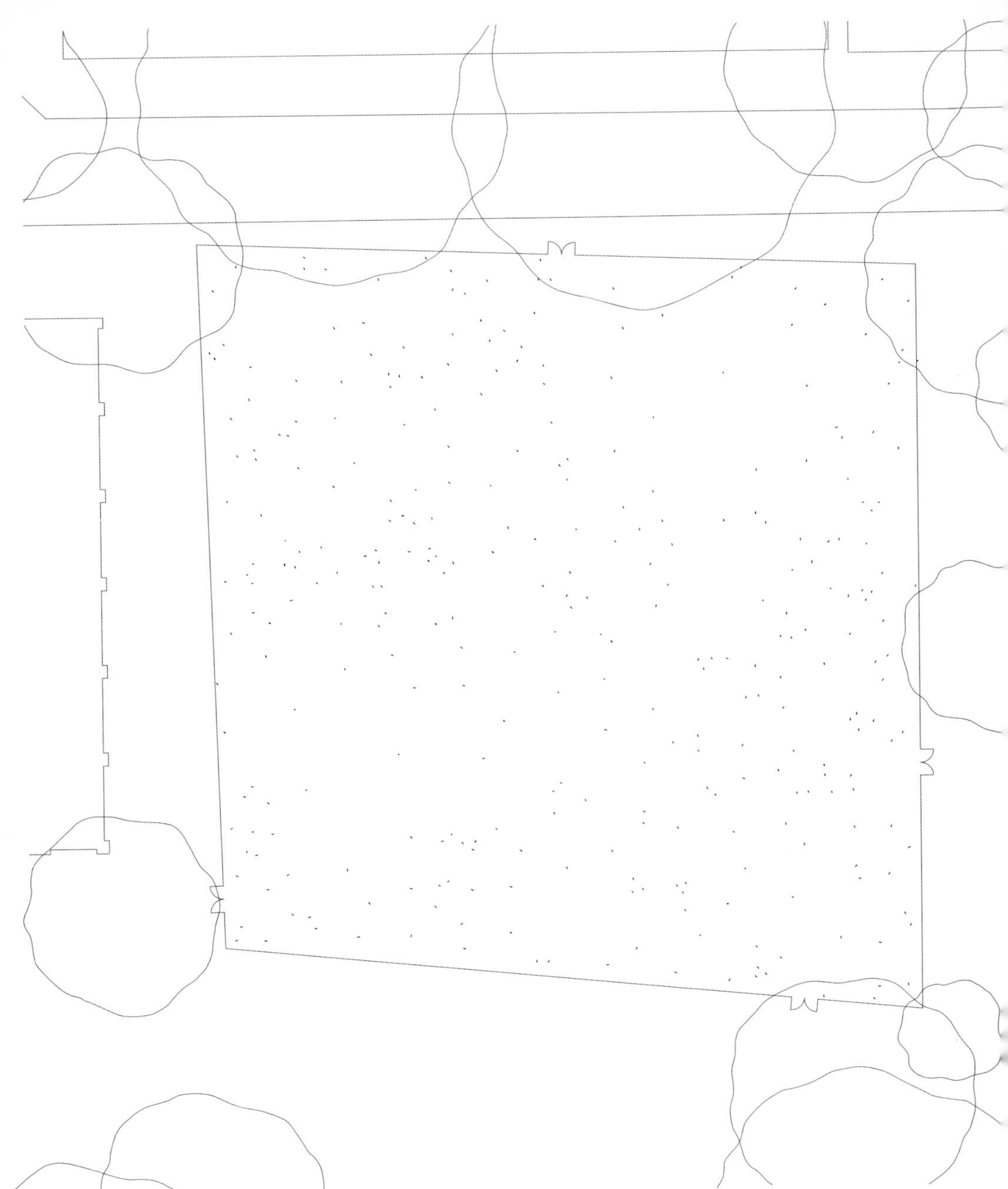

Ground floor plan

DELIVERY ENTRANCE
SMALL WORK SPACE
LAVATORY
PERSONAL WORK SPACE
PASSAGE
MULTIWORK SPACE
WORK SPACE
WORK SPACE
SMALL REST SPACE
BENCH
IRON POT SPACE
MOVABLE SHELF
COMPUTER SPACE
LAVATORY
WORK SPACE
ANAGEMENT SPACE
PRINTER SPACE
MOLDING SPACE
REST SPACE
MACHINE WORK SPACE
WORK SPACE
REST SPACE
SMALL REST SPACE
MULTIWORK SPACE
PERSONAL WORK SPACE
MOVABLE SHELF
BIG WORK TABLE
RELAX SPACE
BENCH
WORK SPACE
MOVABLE SHELF
EXTENSIVE WORK SPAACE
ACE
SHOP SPACE
MAKING MACHINE SPACE
WORK SPACE
MOVABLE SHELF
PASSAGE
RECEPTION
EXHIBITION SPACE
WORK SPACE
PERSONAL WORK SPACE
PROJECTOR SPACE
ENTRANCE HALL
MODELING MACHINE SPACE
SUB ENTRANCE HALL
CIRCULAR SAWING MACHINE SPACE
SAWING MACHINE SPACE
MILLING MACHINE SPACE
DOBILING MACHINE
LOBBY
TURNING MACHINE SPACE
WOODWORKING MACHINE SPACE
DOBILING MACHINE

rt Export Tools Window Help
09-1方向調整070204-3'/070203-2ベース試験（模型により位置調整）（ショップ位置変更）
COM: BG: AA: AREA: TRI: COL: 3 in 10 x
rt Export Tools Window Help
11-2方向調整070204-3'/070203-2ベース試験（模型により位置調整）（ショップ位置変更）
COM: BG: AA: AREA: TRI: COL: in

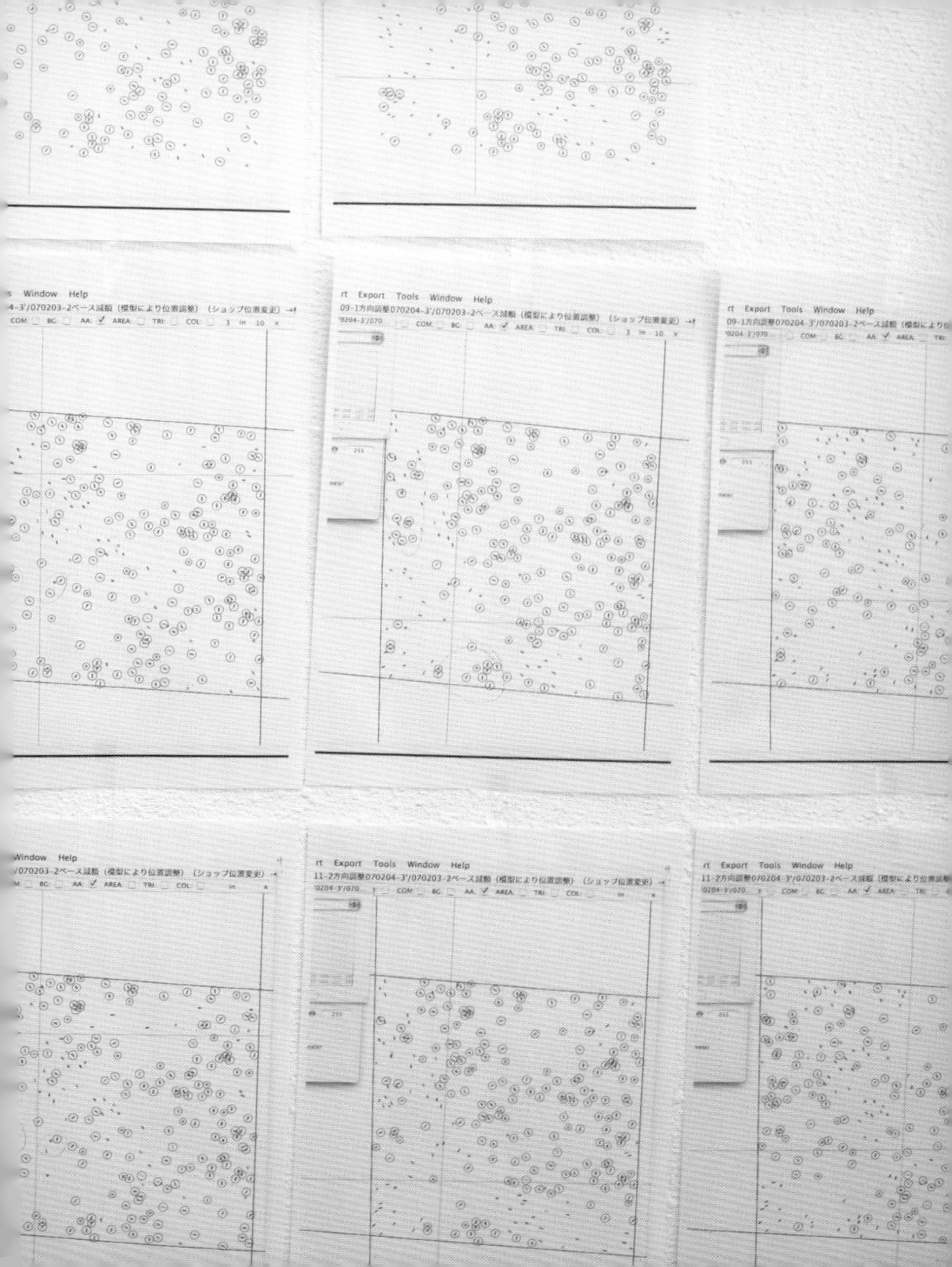

Export Tools Window Help
COM: BG: AA: AREA: TRI: COL: 3 in 10 x

is and following pages
oposal for a weekend house
a young client

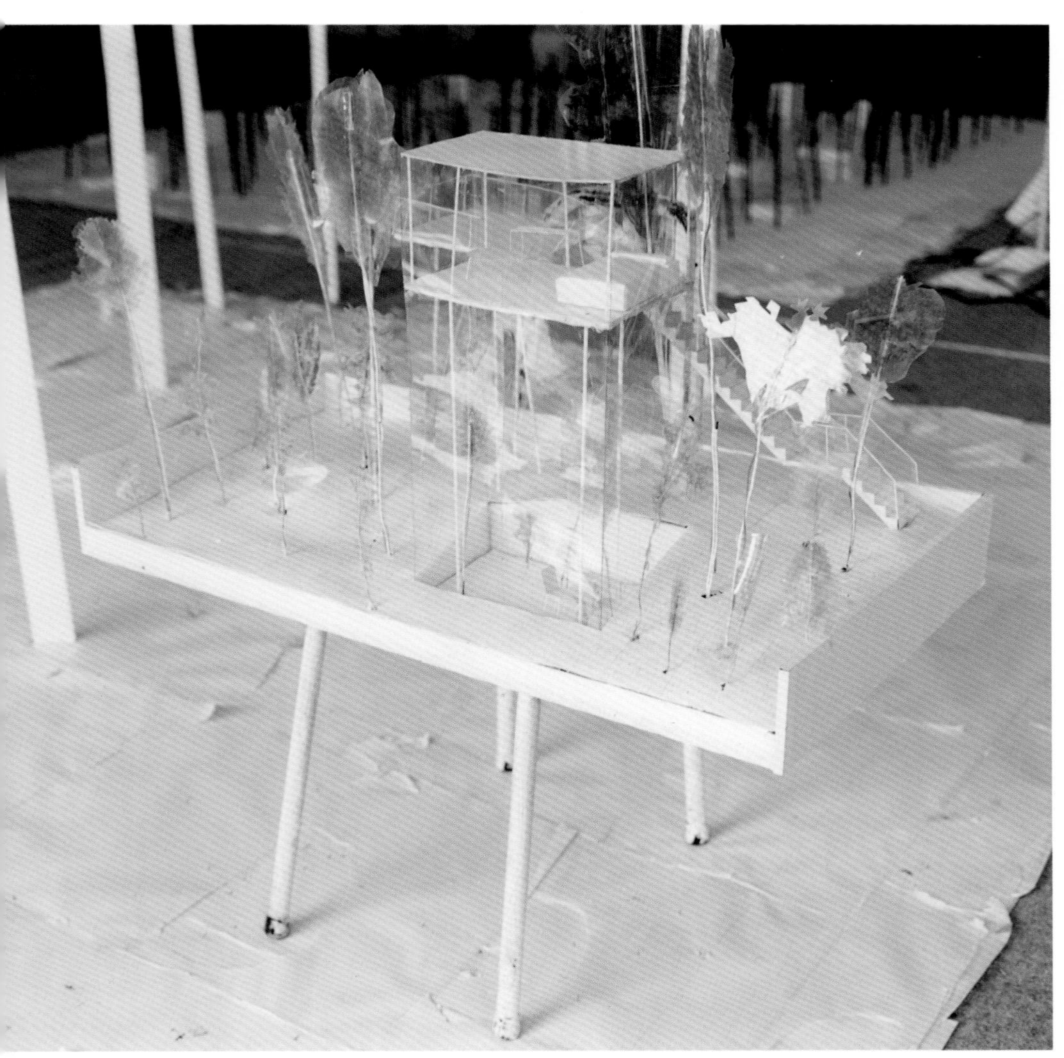

Ryue Nishizawa

kyo – the largest city in the world today – seems to a laboratory for experimentation and innovation in omestic architecture. To some extent the architects your generation working in Japan appear to be re-fining what it means to inhabit the contemporary city. ur design for the Moriyama Houses is at the fore-ont of this process of experimentation, not only ar-itecturally but also in terms of the relationships it es-blishes between its inhabitants and their neighbours. 'as it your intention to engage in a form of 'social en-neering through architecture'?

Actually, to some extent it was. I had a very spe-ic objective for this project, and that was to prove at it is possible to increase the degree of contact be-een public and private space in the city. One of the ost evident characteristics of Tokyo's urban fabric is tendency towards hyper-fragmentation, and I've no-ed that this goes hand in hand with a rising sense architectural introversion. As dwellings become ore introspective people feel less safe in the streets, d public space gradually deadens. Yet living in a city largely about feeling at home in public spaces, mov-g around, walking to the station, going to school and on. Daily life is spread over the city. I'm concerned the increasing enclosure of buildings, so on a very tuitive level I wanted to use this project to experiment th a more permeable form of dwelling. When I start-out I didn't really know what I was going to end up th, though.

The ultimate architectural embodiments of intro-rsion, of course, are the gated communities and for-ied dwellings typical of societies where the gap be-een rich and poor is extreme.

Luckily it's not that bad here. We're fortunate in pan in that there is almost no class system. To some tent, we all consider ourselves the same. There are or and rich, but not entire classes of super poor and per rich.

The area surrounding the Moriyama Houses is a rticularly close society – everybody knows one oth-. There is a distinct sense of community. Tokyo is sentially a conurbation of villages... You feel like u're in a village that extends out into the city. It's ite surprising when you consider that it's the world's largest metropolis – but it's exactly this sense of community permeating the city that made it possible to realise the Moriyama Houses.

I was told that this hyper-fragmentation of the urban fabric, the very phenomenon that defines Japan's great metropolitan sprawl, is continuing even today as the result of heirs dividing up plots to avoid paying inheritance taxes. In an article in Domus, *Akira Suzuki suggested, light-heartedly, that the Moriyama Houses replicate this process at a comically accelerated pace.*

What I wanted to do was clarify this process of fragmentation and embody it into the design. Tokyo's urban geography is reminiscent of a natural landscape – it certainly doesn't look as though it was designed. I don't think this is unique to Japan – there are other parts of Asia where this could happen – but for sure it's very different from any European city. A lot of people find it ugly, and of course compared to some parts of Paris it's not that beautiful; but I'm very interested in the possibilities that could emerge from a design strategy that engages this kind of micro-urbanism.

How does the Moriyama complex work?

The client of the development is Moriyama-san, the owner of the 290-square-metre plot. He lives in one of the apartments in the complex, and the others are occupied by six rental tenants, mostly students or young professionals in their twenties. Building other apartments on the site was a way of generating some income to help pay back the mortgage needed to finance the scheme. Initially, I considered the idea of building much larger volumes, but it did not seem appropriate for the area. This is a very old residential neighbourhood that was developed after the Second World War and in many respects it hasn't changed much since then. People's way of life around there is still very open, and they use the street and their own gardens indifferently. There's a relationship of continuity between building and garden, and that is why I decided to separate the programme into individual functions and scatter them across the entire site, with patios or small gardens between them. Even though they are very close together, each house has

Moriyama Houses
Architects: office of Ryue Nishizawa
Location: Tokyo
Site area: 290.07 sqm
Building area: 130.09 sqm
Total floor area: 263.32 sqm
Structure: steel panels
Principal use: private residence, rental house

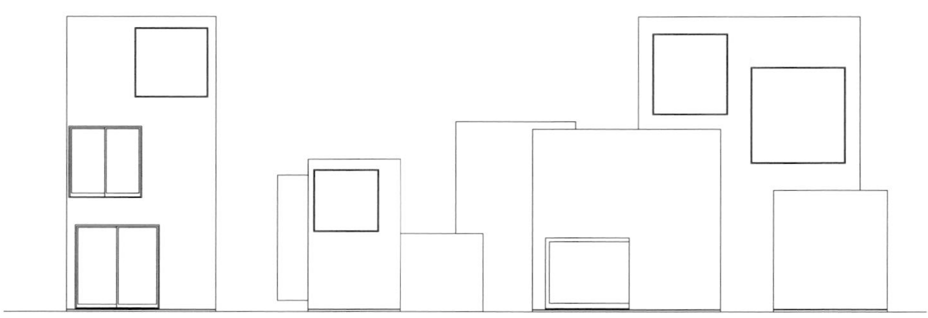

East elevation

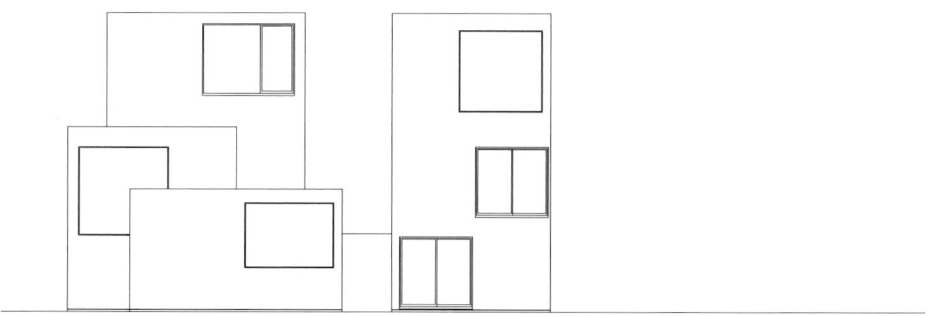

North elevation

Ground floor plan

its own garden so the inhabitants can enjoy not only the interior but also the exterior, and this creates a more open daily life. Anybody can walk through the site: the boundaries are implicit more than physical.

The distribution of the volumes across the site appears to be very carefully considered. Did you arrange the openings so as to give each tenant as much privacy as possible, given the proximity of the various dwellings?

To some extent I did, but the buildings are still very transparent. The funny thing is, though, that the existing neighbour's apartments are even more transparent! Here there are very different social customs with respect to Europe: every part of the dwelling is visible from the street, not just the living room. There is a female tenant who lives in one of the Moriyama apartments and sleeps with the curtains open – anyone who walks past can see her through the large glass window.

So the visual permeability of the apartments has very little effect on people's behaviour?

It took time for their lifestyle to adapt to this transparent atmosphere, but now they seem well adjusted. In some cases they installed curtains. I actually rather like these individual contributions to the building – the little ways in which people make spaces their own.

One of the amazing things about Tokyo is the wa it succeeds in preserving so many village-like neig bourhoods made up of tiny dwellings and integrate them seamlessly into a vast metropolis. How do yo think this is possible? What is Tokyo's relationship t this issue of scale?

The impression of disorder that visitors perceive Tokyo is actually an illusion – in many ways it is an i credibly efficient city. Vast numbers of people mov across it every day, the transportation infrastructu works well and there is very little crime. On the dow side, though, there is very little public space that isn functional to consumption in one way or the other, e ther as part of a shopping mall or occupied by cafés an restaurants. One has to be disciplined to move aroun Tokyo without spending money at each corner.

How are the great Japanese architects of the pos war period perceived by your generation of designers Do you see your concerns and methodologies as be ing related in any way?

The reality that the post-war architects had to de with was very harsh, and their approach was in man ways quite heavy-handed as a consequence. I thir the younger generation has a lighter touch and is muc freer in its expression, in part due to the more vers tile technologies and materials at our disposal today.

e bedroom window of one of the units in
e Moriyama Houses complex. A recess
tween the ground and the base of the
alls creates the illusion that the boxes are
spended

The bathroom of Mr Moriyama, the client and one of the tenants. Several of the boxes in the complex are mono-functional and disconnected from the others

Mr Moriyama in his kitchen

The Tezuka family

kaharu + Yui Tezuka (Tezuka Architects, Tokyo)

ur first building to be widely published was the Roof use, a very small family house that effectively used roof as a living room. Your most recent design, a nt kindergarten for almost six hundred children, us- the roof as a playground. What is it that fascinates u so much about roofs?

I guess you could call us roof architects. If you nk about it, there aren't many other architects work- so extensively with the possible uses of the roof face at the moment. It's like a whole new territory be discovered, colonised and made habitable. The ojects you mention have given us a lot of visibility in pan and abroad, but in fact the roof is only a part of r interests, one of many concepts and strategies we e to explore.

Can you describe the Fuji Kindergarten project?

The brief was to design a private kindergarten build- capable of accommodating 540 children to replace d expand an existing one. It's a very well-known hool in Tokyo: the quality of education is considered be exceptionally high, and some people commute o hours to bring their children here. The budget we ere working with wasn't large, about four million dol- s, so it's actually quite a simple building. The class- oms are arranged in a doughnut-shaped ring, a bit like lying saucer, surrounding a central playground. The tire ring is free of partitions – there are no divisions tween the classrooms – and the sliding doors that parate the classrooms from the playground can be pt open for eight months of the year, so there is nazing spatial continuity throughout the building. We vised a modular system comprised of 3,000 light- eight wooden boxes that could be used to create nporary partitions and adapt the space for various us- without having to erect permanent walls. Part of e brief was to preserve the trees growing on the e. To do this we had to be very careful not to dam- e the roots, so we couldn't put down normal foun- tions. We devised a way of 'floating' the building on e site without interfering at all with the roots. It was portant to us that these very ancient trees should be- me part of the building, so we built around them and ned the trunks into a part of the classrooms. The up- r limbs protrude through the roof-deck, making them more accessible so children can climb them. When the leaves come out they cast a wonderful shadow onto the playground. The height of the ceiling in the class- rooms is 2.5 metres, which is the lowest we could legally make it in a school. We designed the building to be seen from the perspective of a five-year old child, so everything is very low. The roof deck has a slight in- ward camber both to allow the rain to flow off and to give the children better grip when they're running. You don't really notice it – it's only a gradient of 1:30 – but it's important. Another imperceptible detail is that the plan isn't a geometrically perfect oval – I drew two cir- cles by hand, and we scanned them and traced them off to create a plan. This means that the depth of the classrooms varies quite a lot from one side to the oth- er. There's something about these small irregularities that actually makes the space much more human at a subconscious level.

Do you think it's critically important for the kinder- garten to be so large for the ring concept to work?

I think it could be smaller, but it wouldn't be as im- pressive. The remarkable thing about this building is that it allows over five hundred children to interact freely without ever seeming crowded. Also, if the school were smaller the children wouldn't get as varied a cur- riculum – here they do painting classes, learn music, learn to do gardening and so on. They even have a pen with some sheep. We were struck quite deeply by one of the things our client, the principal, told us: he said he wants to create 'future nostalgia' in the children, a memory of a time when they were truly happy.

Do you envision this building having the twenty- or thirty-year life span typical of so many constructions in Japan?

No – I'm actually deeply contrary to the culture of disposable buildings. A short-intended life span is of- ten an excuse to build poor-quality architecture that doesn't work well even for the short time it exists. I al- so think there's some mythology in this idea that Japan- ese architecture has always been short-lived – my grandfather's house is over a hundred years old and is still standing. The only reason why the others are not is because they were torn down, certainly not because

Fuji Kindergarten
Architects: Tezuka Architects
Total floor area: 1,304 sqm
Structure: steel frame
Contractors: Takenaka Corporation
Year of completion: 2006

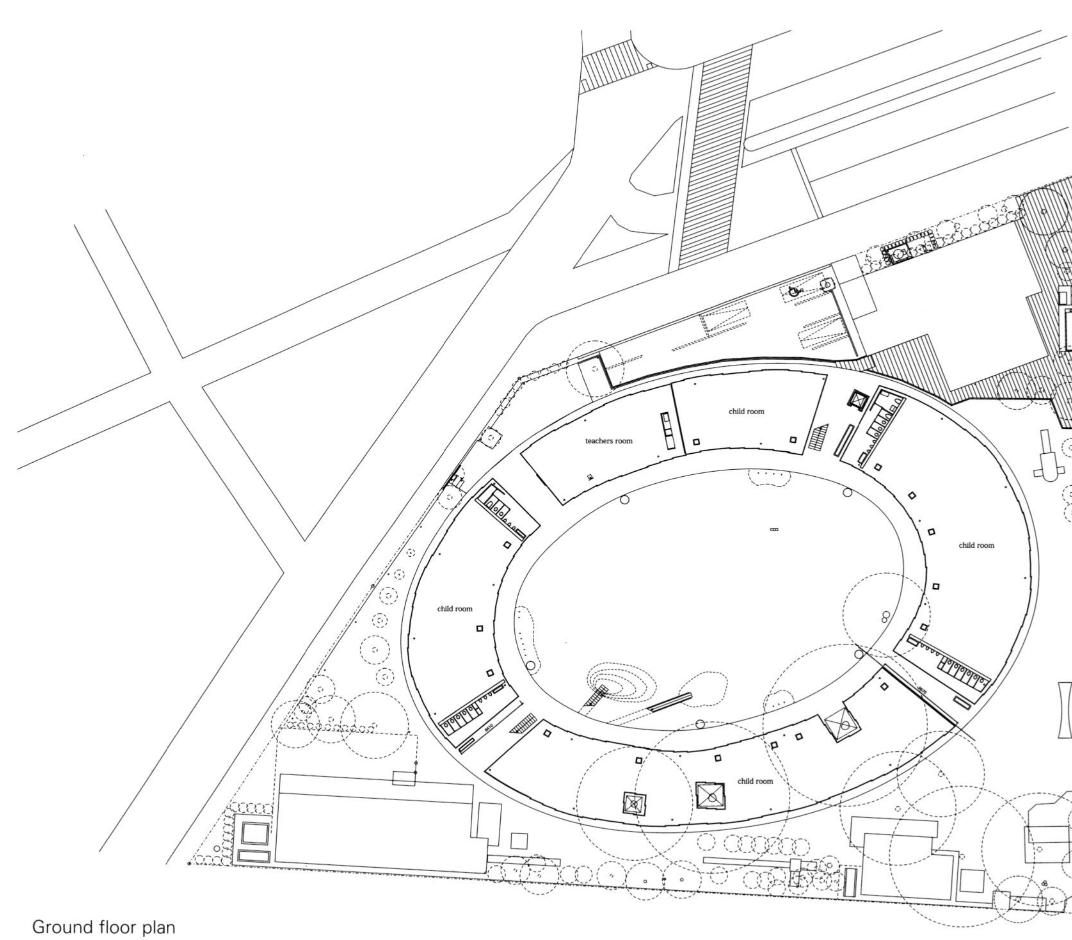

Ground floor plan

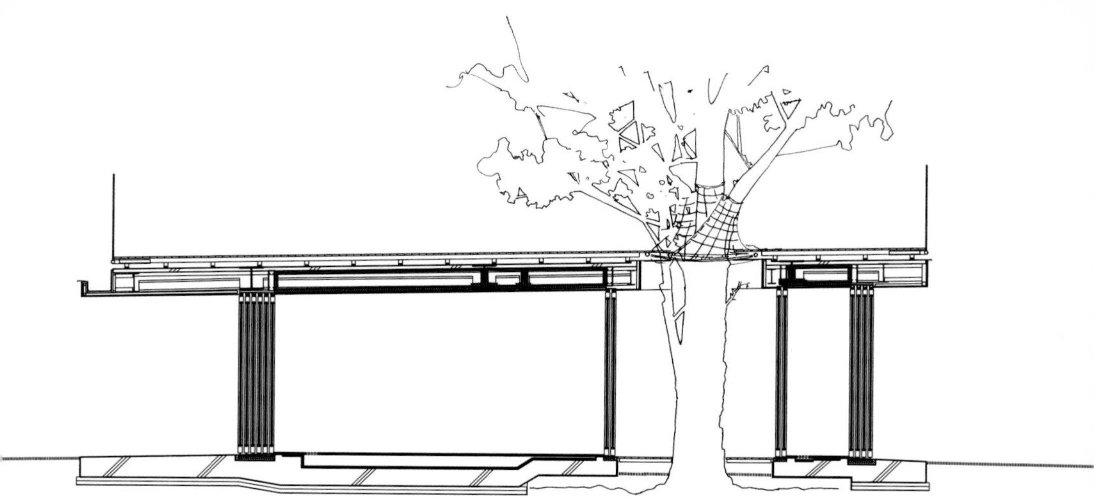

ction

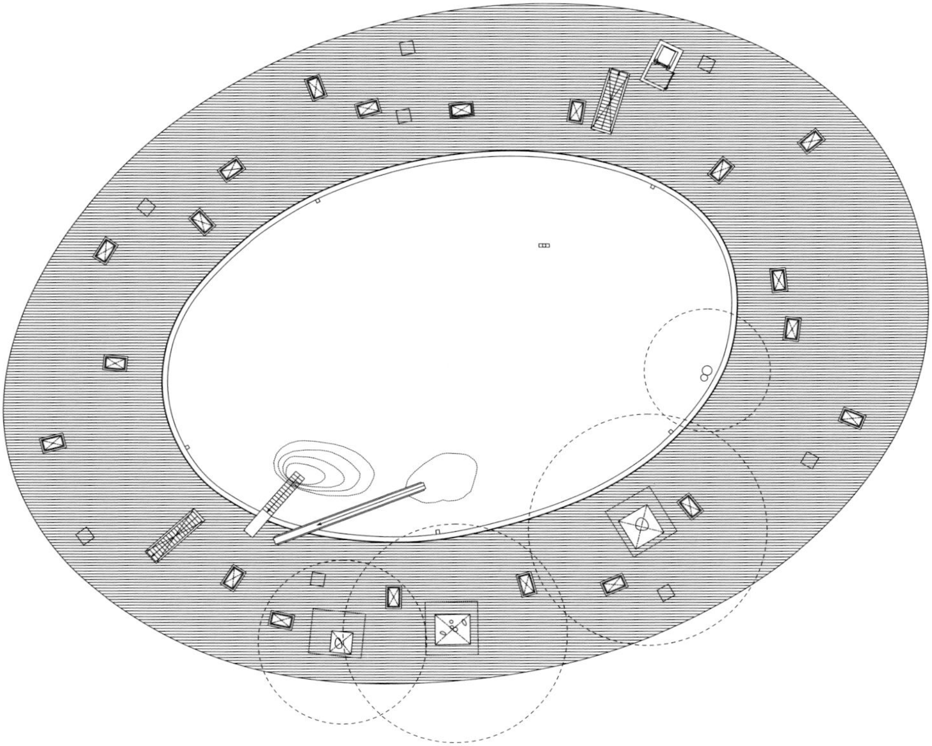

of plan

of a lack of quality in the craftsmanship. My father was an architect, so I've been surrounded by these issues since I was a small child, and I've seen a radical change in culture over the decades. The architects of the post-war era weren't designing buildings for a twenty-year life span. It's a much newer phenomenon than that.

Having studied architecture in the US and then worked for Richard Rogers in London, how do you see yourself professionally? Do you consider yourself a foreigner or a local in the Japanese context?

The principles of Japanese architecture are a subconscious presence in my mind – I don't need to consciously think about them. This is perhaps one of the things that differentiate my generation from the previous one – one of the main preoccupations of architects like Fumihiko Maki, who studied abroad and returned to Japan, was how to successfully amalgamate Japaneseness and Modernism. There was a desire to create something new, but still Japanese, and maybe this is what Kenzo Tange and that whole generation was aiming for too. However, I'm not sure my feeling is shared by other members of the younger generation, because architecturally speaking I'm an outsider, I'm not considered to be from Japan.

Can you say something about the way your generation perceives its relationship with politics?

Architects of the post-war period were very aware of architecture's political dimension and struggled to assert an understanding of architecture as a way in which societies define their physical identities and express their ideals. I don't think that's the case for my generation – perhaps we feel that we have less role to play in politics, or we're wary of placing too much responsibility on architecture to avoid the disillusionment that followed the excessive optimism of the past.

So you feel the battle has already been won?

To some extent, yes. The battle of the post-war generation probably has. They had the task of establishing the position of the architect in a society that until recently didn't even know the meaning of the word 'architect'. Nowadays if you go to any convenience store you'll find five or six magazines just about houses. T architect has never been held in such high regard Japanese history. There are innumerable TV p grammes about architecture – a Japanese TV chan is actually shooting a documentary about us at the m ment. Nowadays architecture is considered a 'sa subject for TV programmes, one that will guarant you an audience. A week ago we held the official op ing of the kindergarten, and more than fifteen TV p grammes called in wanting to cover the event. We h to stop answering the phone because we were getti too many calls.

From what you are saying, it sounds as thou Japan is even more deeply invested than the West the culture of 'starchitecture'...

It is, but with an important difference. In Europe the architects the journalists chase. Here they cha architecture. It's quite common that people don't member the name of the architect but of the buildi A lot of people will be familiar with the Roof House the Fuji Kindergarten, but have never heard of us. La week there was a huge photo of the kindergarten the front page of a national daily, which was great, b interestingly there was no mention of the archite They even listed the construction company, but n us! The same thing happened with a Japanese in-flig magazine – they put one of our buildings on the cov but didn't mention us anywhere. This is very differe from the West, where it's the architects rather than t buildings that have a cult following. The exception, course, is Tadao Ando – his face is even more pu lished than his buildings.

What do you see as your role in a society whe the architect's work potentially receives so much tention?

Despite all the disillusionment of the past, I do b lieve it's possible to improve the condition of socie through architecture. What's important is that it mu retain contact with people and their everyday existen Actually, the only thing that remains constant in arc tecture is everyday life. That, above all, is what w want to work with.

mo wrestling in the kindergarten's playground

ith over five hundred children, Fuji ndergarten is the largest in Japan. It is so pular that a number of parents commute nost two hours to allow their children attend

Fuji

e idea of using the Fuji Kindergarten's of as an additional playground was spired by a previous project by Tezuka chitects, the Roof House

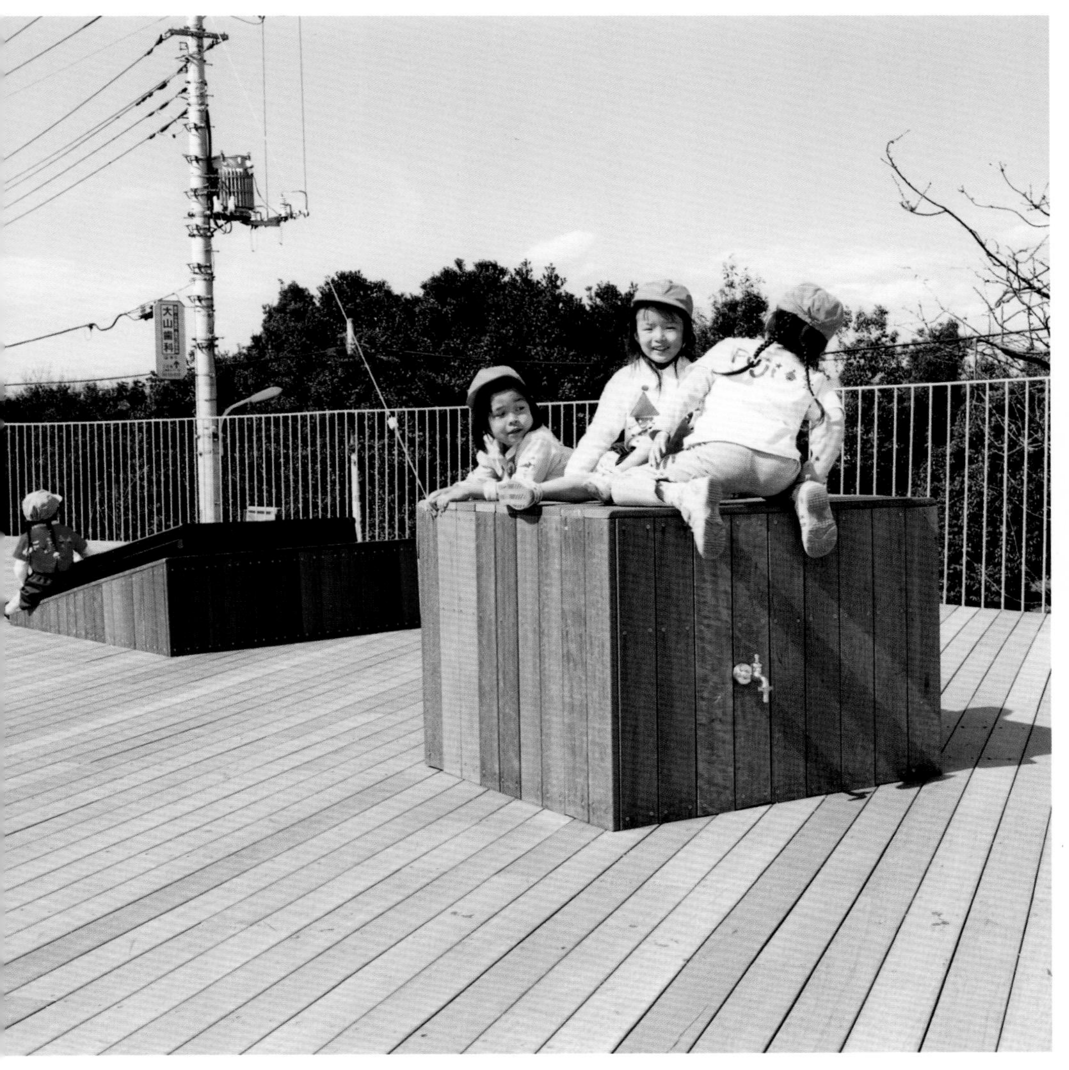

An interior and exterior façade of sliding doors means that in the summer all barriers between interior and exterior can be removed, transforming the entire site into a continuous, unobstructed space

The preservation of trees existing on the site became an important theme of the kindergarten's design. By integrating them into the design, they became a central feature of the roof/playground

Yoshiharu Tsukamoto and Momoyo Kaijima

oking at the projects your office is working on at the oment, it's clear that you're making a shift from the ale of the dwelling towards the urban scale. In the roduction to Post-Bubble City *you describe the velling as a 'maquette' for something larger. The im- cation is that even large urban projects with public ogrammes can be designed and understood along the me lines as dwellings. Could you tell us about this ncept of the public building as dwelling?*

The first public building we designed was a rea- nably large landscape museum and a cultural centre. e initiator of this project was a landscape designer no asked us to design a 'house' that was totally con- cted to the park according to the principles of 'parki- cture', a concept originating in the US in the 1970s, hink. The whole rooftop was to be covered with an cessible garden, so we proposed to install an undu- ed roof supported by fifteen hollow cylinders, each ntaining a room with a different function: offices, cture spaces, storage, toilets and so on. The space tween the cylinders was kept open and was fur- shed with a mobile café, library, shops and so on. The per parts of the cylinders stick through the roof-plate d work as plant-pots so that trees can be grown on e roof. Our intention with this project was to design ch cylinder as an individual 'house' – in this way we uld break the architecture down to the domestic ale and tackle a kind of 'microurbanism' comprising teen houses with specific functions arranged under single roof. If we were to receive the right commis- on, I believe this is a concept that we could develop rther.

There are very few obvious similarities that connect ur generation of Japanese architects with the previ- s one – certainly fewer than in Europe and America, here a generational divide is also apparent, but there a clearer sense of continuity. Very little seems to re- ain today of the Metabolist and post-Metabolist eras the work being done here today... Did some kind of nerational fracture take place in Japan?

Today's architectural scene in Japan is more relat- to Shinohara than to the Metabolists. I was the last udent of Shinohara, and my professor, Sakamoto, as one of Shinohara's most distinguished followers. ter the Second World War Shinohara broke away om the Metabolists, accusing them of becoming too reaucratic and technocratic, and created his own architectural current with Arata Isozaki. The awareness of identity and individuality had been totally lost in the context of Metabolism, so Isozaki and Shinohara reaffirmed the importance of poetry and individuality in the creation of architecture in the Japanese scene in the 1960s. Toyo Ito was part of this effort, too. Ito worked for Kikutake, one of the most famous members of the Metabolist movement, but was disappointed with him and his experience in Kikutake's office, and ended up turning to Shinohara. Ito learned a huge amount from him. Kazuyo Sejima was also in Ito's staff, and Jun Aoki worked for Isozaki, so it's evident that Shinohara and Isozaki influenced an entire generation.

It's interesting to notice that if you consider all the young practices at work today in this city, each regenerating a small grain of Tokyo, it's a form of Metabolism. So as a group, one could say that we are effectively carrying out the work of the Metabolists in a progressive, piecemeal fashion.

Atelier Bow-Wow is one of the best-known Japanese practices abroad, but your architecture is the opposite of the iconic formalism that normally makes architects internationally successful: it's much more focused on ideas and programme than on creating form. Do you ever feel the temptation to move towards a more formal language? Can an architect work today while actively negating the concept of 'style', as you do?

I think so. The challenge we face is to continue working through a very individual approach without succumbing to the need for an iconic image. I'm very interested in anonymous buildings and vernacular buildings – even new vernacular buildings – but we have no interest in 'heroic' architecture. It's an aversion that comes from very deep inside. My interest is to tap into or participate in the production of 'lively' space. I'm not as interested in distinguishing between big and small as between lively and dead. *Pet Architecture* and *Made in Tokyo* can be seen as studies of good forms of urban practice inside Tokyo, and many of the buildings in them are very lively despite not having any iconic architectural design. I'm not sure why I have insisted on this point for so long, but I definitely have a very strong interest in this concept of 'lively' space. I'm also highly interested in the quality of public space in Japan: it's very different from that of Western countries. I think the quality of Japanese public space is something that arises from a mix between domesticity and

House & Atelier Bow-Wow
Architects: Atelier Bow-Wow
Location: Shinjuku-ku, Tokyo
Site area: 109.03 sqm
Building area: 59.76 sqm
Total floor area: 211.27 sqm
Structure: reinforced concrete and steel frame

Second floor

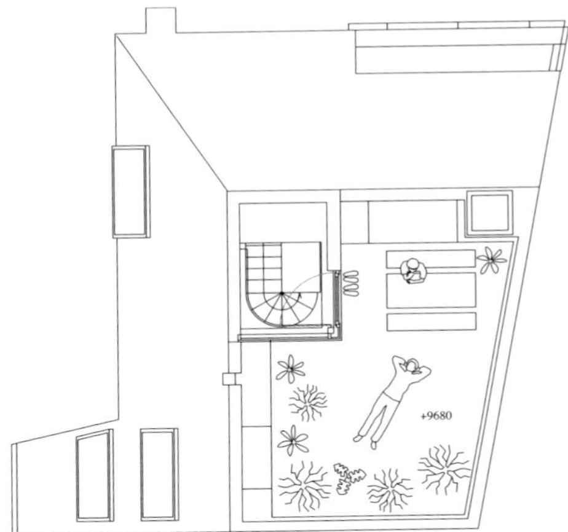

Roof plan

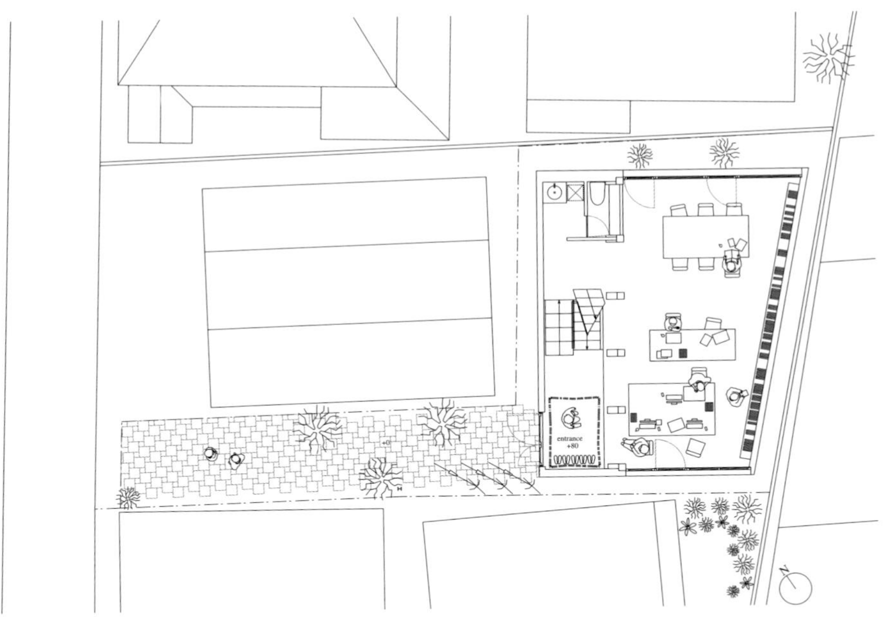

Ground floor site plan

YAMAHA
品川C い
72-24

Sectional perspective

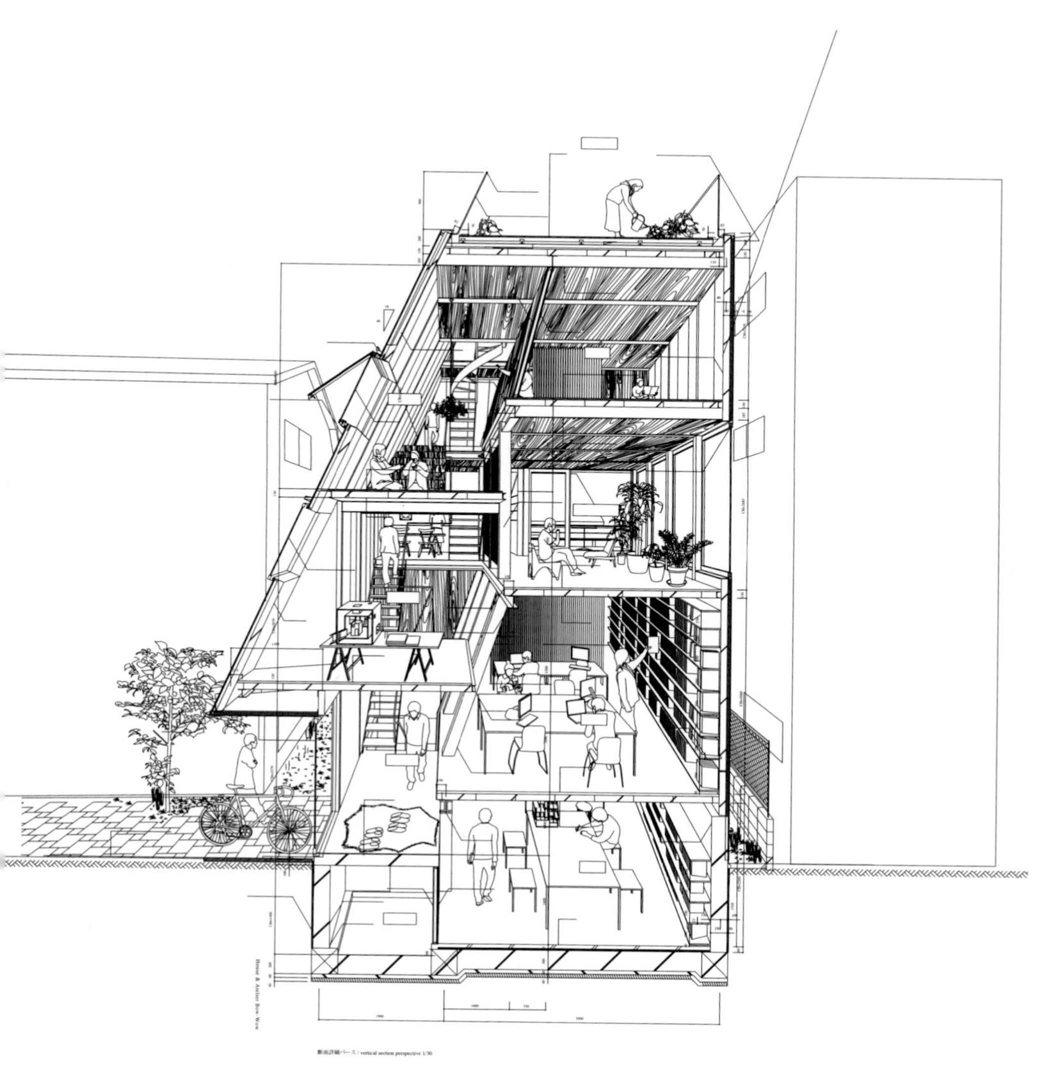

断面詳細パース / vertical section perspective 1/30

京

pp. 230–35
House & Atelier Bow-Wow's upper floors are occupied by the living quarters the couple designed for themselves. Although the building is almost invisible from the exterior, it enjoys extensive views of the surrounding area.

Opposite
The ground floor and basement are occupied by the offices of the couple's architecture practice, Atelier Bow-Wow

micro-commerce – domesticity is a very important quality in the Japanese city. In Tokyo you can observe a lot of examples of what could be described as the invasion of domesticity into the public or the commercial realm, and I don't think in the history of architecture such a phenomenon has occurred anywhere else. I have the intuition there is something new and fascinating in this blurring of domesticity and public space, something that's worth investigating, although it's not yet quite clear what it might be.

Earlier you were describing one of your recent projects, the Mado Building, as an attempt to subvert the assumption that the canonical office building must be made of glass.

The Mado Building was a strange commission in that it was designed without a specific programme. The developer intended to sell it immediately after it was completed, so our brief was to design an 'attractive' building with generic functionality. The site is quite unusual – it's a triangular peninsula belonging to a commercial district that juts into a residential neighbourhood. It's surrounded by apartments, most of which look down onto the site. I wanted to take this opportunity to propose a new typology for this kind of commercial building. A number of commercial buildings are clad in glass curtain walls, which makes them very anonymous, and in many cases the tenants aren't good at using this kind of transparent buildings – they put shelves against transparent walls, which defeats the whole point of the transparency. So we decided to work with windows – *mado* means window, so this is a 'window-building'. The shape is defined by the projected shadow-lines, giving it a polyhedric form. Having derived a shape for the building, we started positioning the windows, placing three façades onto the street to make three continuous surfaces with a chequered pattern of solids and voids. Once we had established this chequered texture, we subverted it by stretching and compressing the openings so as to give the outer skin a more irregular appearance. The largest window is 2.2 by 3.3 metres, the largest standard size double-glazing available in Japan.

Perhaps you could tell us something about the Tower House, your most recent residential project.

We were commissioned to design the Tower House on a tiny site in a very densely populated area of Tokyo, so our only option was to build vertically, which inspire us to give it a watchtower-like appearance. The si measures 4 by 9 metres, and the actual footprint of tl building is only 3 by 6 metres. The overall height 11.5 metres, which is the highest we could go with th setback from the street. Given the very small footprir the proportions of the living room are quite vertic and it is connected to the other floors by a suspende staircase that dissects the house. The clients are u ing the basement as extra storage space, but it cou be employed also as an extra bedroom.

Several of the architects we have met since arri ing in Tokyo have expressed frustration with the fa that much of their work consists of small houses. Yo on the other hand, seem to have turned the proce of designing dwellings into a means of observing ar engaging the urban fabric of Tokyo and other citie One could say that the collective body of your domest designs forms an unwritten manifesto for your visi of the city. Since 1990, you have carried out innume able small projects, few of which can be described spectacular, but each of which has a precise and uniq programmatic objective.

I think this body of work constitutes the foundatior of a manifesto that speaks of how we see the futur We are very interested in architecture as a languag in the concept of communicating through architectur In each project we try to reinterpret the way a buildir 'behaves' in its context – you could describe it as process of destabilisation of the clichés or stereotype that surround architecture. I think the big challenge f architects in the twenty-first century is to reinvent th concept of urbanity: in the twentieth century we bu a lot of buildings but didn't really consider their colle tive impact on our daily routines. There is a sense repetition, especially in contemporary domestic arch tecture, but there is very little sense of 'citiness', of u banity: our objective is to rediscover what is excitir about our cities. It's the only thing we can do, since w can't expect to rebuild Tokyo from scratch, and neith would we want to. We have to re-evaluate the qua ties of existing architecture, and designing small buil ings can be an amazing way of conducting observatior on residential neighbourhoods.

I'm working on two issues now: how to preserv the existing urban fabric and how to create new a chitecture that functions successfully in the conte

Tower House
Architects: Atelier Bow-Wow
Location: Shinagawa-ku, Tokyo
Site area: 42.29 sqm
Building area: 18.44 sqm
Total floor area: 65.28 sqm
Structure: reniforced concrete

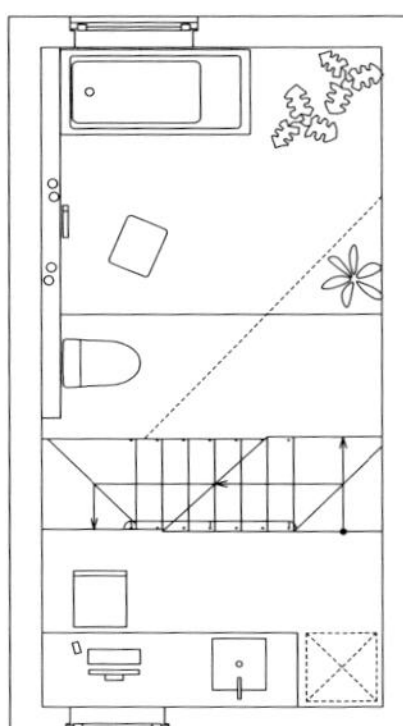

Third floor

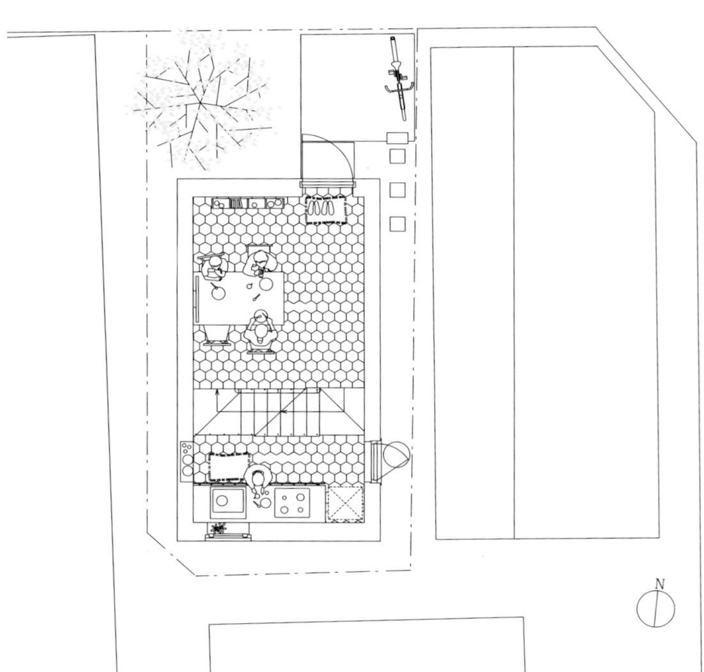

Ground floor plan

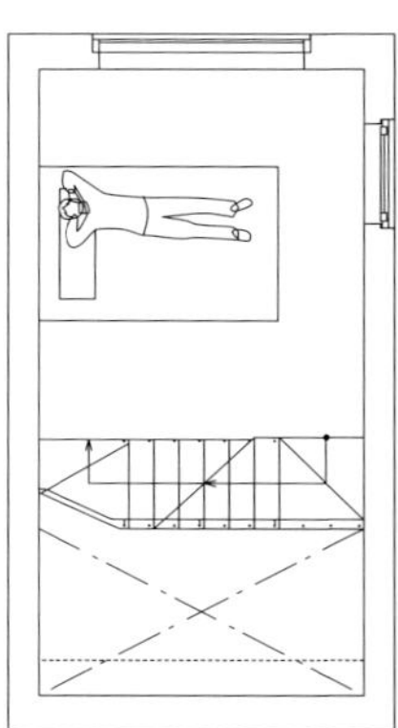

Second floor

ctional perspective

of the existing fabric. We're particularly interested in cities such as Tokyo that are composed largely of detached houses, because on a global scale they are quite rare. The amazing thing about this kind of urbanism is that even very central parts of the city such as the area where my office is located retain some of the qualities of a village. There is a subtlety and variety in the scale that derives from a very intimate relationship between individuals and their houses, sedimenting in microscopic transformations and adaptations that take place over time. This kind of fabric is under threat, but there's no reason why it shouldn't continue to exist.

Today we are increasingly confronted by the regeneration of this type of fabric built in the 1950s and 1960s. At that time people didn't care much about long-term development, so many of the buildings were erected with relatively short life spans in mind. To be able to preserve such an environment for as long as possible we need to understand the principles of 'citiness' that produced it in the first place. Each building is the evaluation of the existing context and the existing situation.

Are you advocating longer-life-span buildings than those constructed in the post-war era?

That's part of the argument, but actually there's no simple solution. We have to face the problem of regeneration and modernisation in these neighbourhoods, but at the same time we need to do what we can to preserve what exists. Why is the kind of architectural language we use so important? Because the 1960s, when the Metabolists emerged, was the decade when the city was developing fastest, largely on greenfield sites. It was the time for large, visionary construction projects, massive infrastructure schemes, large capital investments designed according to the precepts of centralised power. Today we are building on urban brownfield sites.
It's very different. In this sense we need to consider a
other type of urbanism, something that perhaps cou
be described as micro-urbanism based on the typolo
and morphology of existing buildings.

*Why are you so strongly in favour of the hype
fragmentary nature of Tokyo's urban fabric? What is
that you like about it?*

Residential areas of this kind are varied, divers
transformational, adaptive. If you look at commerc
neighbourhoods like Roppongi Hills or any of the o
er well-designed business districts, you see that pu
lic space is complete, it's done, it's thick, it's immob
and incapable of adapting. It cannot include small bu
ness and it's entirely occupied by shops owned
chains. It's not capable of hosting small, distinct su
jectivities. Tokyo's residential fabric is much more
ceptive to diversity.

*Tokyo's skyline, particularly in suburban areas, is
markably low compared to other Asian cities. This is pa
ticularly surprising considering how expensive land
here. What are the historical motivations for this?*

After the war some areas were zoned as com
mercial neighbourhoods, and were given a more co
ventionally urban appearance with taller buildings on la
er plots. Others, such as the neighbourhood I live
are comparatively old and retain the urban texture
an era preceding Tokyo's modernisation. The seism
ity of the region has always deterred people from bui
ing vertically, but there is also the existence of a ve
strong tradition of 'one site, one building'. Since the co
struction of the city has been largely dependent on
dividual initiative, the outcome has been an extreme
fragmentary urban fabric, and this process resulted
today's situation in which the value of land is extreme
high and yet the average height of buildings throug
out Tokyo is only 1.5 storeys.

Commissioned by a young couple, the Tower House takes advantage of a small site by maximising its vertical extension

The client in the living room of the Tower House

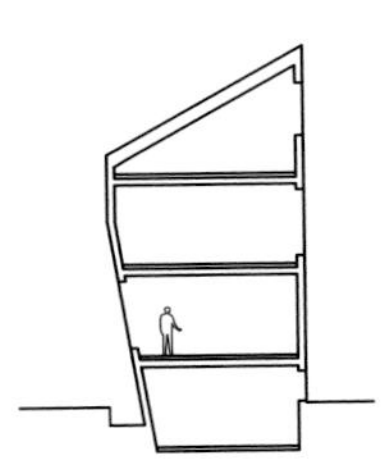

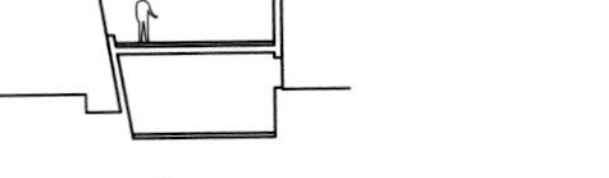

Cross section

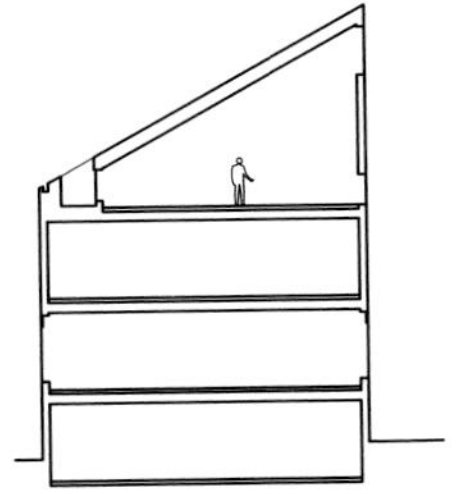

Longitudinal section

Mado Building
Architects: Atelier Bow-Wow
Location: Setagaya, Tokyo
Site area: 191.98 sqm
Building area: 162.1 sqm
Total floor area: 211.27 sqm
Structure: reinforced concrete and steel frame

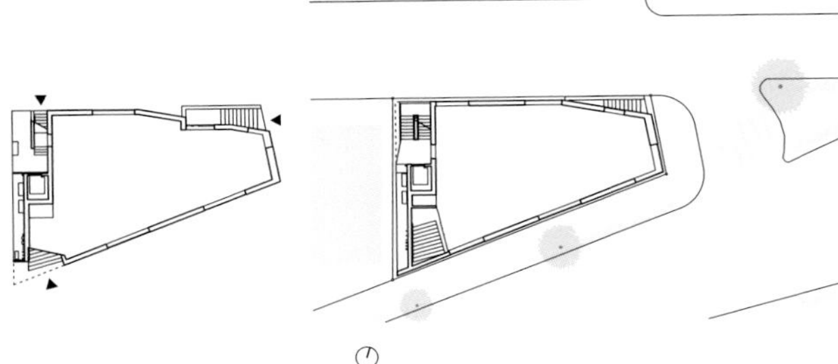

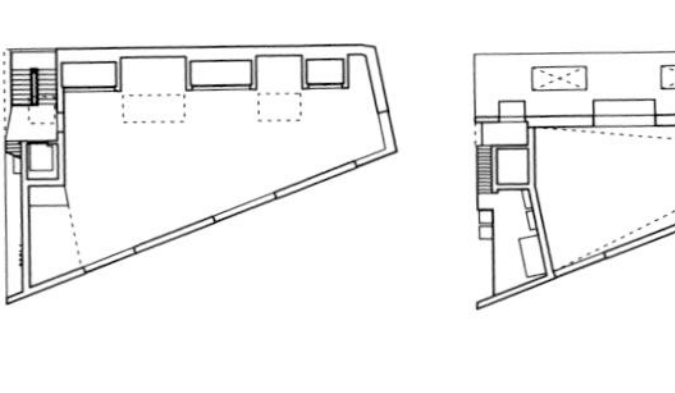

Floor plans

38·98

mirai
crocs
www.crocs.co.jp
小島病院

e Mado Building was designed as an
ernative to the glass curtain wall office
ildings that characterise much of Tokyo.
angular shape was generated by
idying and designing the shadow pattern
vould cast through the seasons

SECOM

Makoto Yokomizo

akoto Yokomizo (AAT+, Tokyo)

'inning the first prize in the Tomihiro Art Museum in-rnational design competition was an important turn-g point for your practice, AAT+, founded only a few ›ars earlier. Could you tell us about this museum?

It was a unique project right from the beginning. ıe brief, in particular, posed an interesting challenge. ›llowing an accident in the 1970s, the Japanese ath-:e Tomihiro Hoshino was paralysed from the neck ›wn, and began to paint watercolours by holding a ush in his mouth. Over time he gained considerable cognition and in 1991 a small museum was opened Azuma, his hometown, to display his work. The ıllery received visitors from all over Japan and proved be a great success, becoming one of the region's ma-attractions.

Eventually the town of Azuma decided to hold an ternational competition for a new museum to house s works. It was a high-profile call for entries: my de-gn was chosen among over 1,200 submissions. I pro-›sed to tightly pack 33 single-storey cylindrical exhi-tion spaces of different diameters into a square plan, ›it like a cluster of soap bubbles. The cylinders range ›m 5 to 16 metres in diameter. Where the cylinders tersect the square footprint they are simply cut off, ıd the leftover spaces between the cylinders form ıht-wells or small gardens. Each of the cylindrical oms would constitute an autonomous exhibition ›ace, reading room, café, and so on. In consultation ıth the artist, we chose a range of colour tones for ıch space taking inspiration from the surrounding land-:ape and from the colours used in his paintings. We anted to create an effect whereby the roof of the useum appears as an abstract form taken from the ırrounding hills.

How does the circulation work in this museum?

Since the museum displays the work of only one tist, and he is still alive today, it was very important engage him as a specific subject. The fact that the tist is in a wheelchair was an important influence: s point of view is lower than most people's, and this as something we took into consideration when de-signing the sight lines through the space. The nature of his work also had to be considered when defining the way visitors would interact with the building. His paintings, mostly watercolours, are extremely fragile, which means they have to be kept in temperature-con-trolled rooms with no natural light. They are also very small, so it required a lot of delicacy to display them effectively. If you look at the paintings randomly, you don't clearly understand the story, so they have to be arranged in a legible order. This was one of the reasons why we chose circular exhibition spaces: each room could be organised as an individual 'capsule' with its own theme and its own logic. We decided this layout would work a lot better than a square plan, in the sense that it's a lot less hierarchical. In a circular space there are no sides and no back – it's an even form that al-lows you to experience the art as a continuous se-quence or flow.

Because the paintings are rather small, it can be-come tiring to observe them continuously for too long. For this reason we decided to alternate gallery spaces with reading spaces, a view over the nearby lake, the café, a souvenir shop and so on. Between the cylinders there are small courtyards with gardens, one of which is accessible to visitors. Our choice of plants for this garden was inspired by the scenes depicted in Tomi-hiro Hoshino's paintings.

Earthquakes aren't uncommon in Azuma. How did you deal with the structural challenges this posed?

Because the plan is comprised of tightly packed cir-cular rooms, it was necessary that the walls of the structure be as light as possible. Most of the self-sup-porting cylinders consist of prefabricated sheet-steel el-ements built by a manufacturer specialised in the con-struction of silos. Three of them have reinforced con-crete walls to give them extra rigidity. The steel walls are 9 mm plates. The cylinders touch in several points, supporting each other and distributing forces, which makes for a highly efficient structural system. Each cylinder structurally complements the others and to-gether they become a rigid framework.

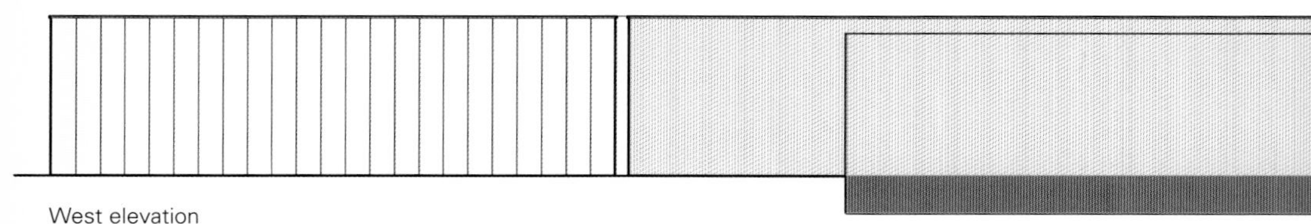
West elevation

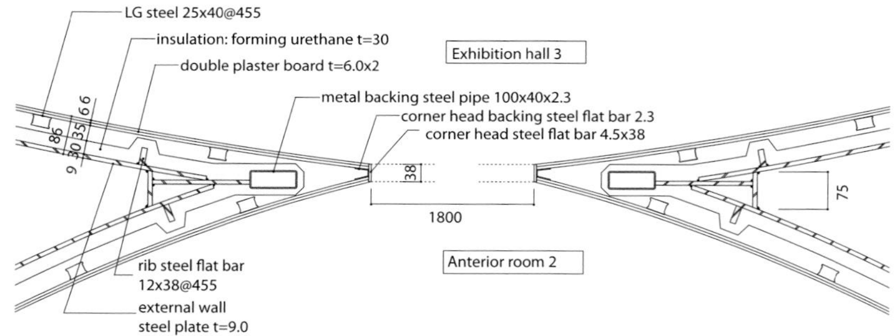

Construction detail: steel cylinders

Tomihiro Art Museum
Architects: AAT+ Makoto Yokomizo Architects Inc.
Client and owner: City of Midori
Structural engineers: Arup Japan
Contractors: Kajima Corporation
Site area: 18,114 sqm
Building area: 2,463 sqm
Total floor area: 2,463 sqm

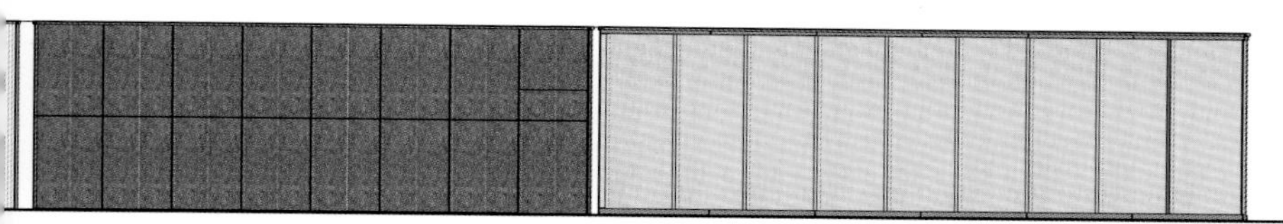

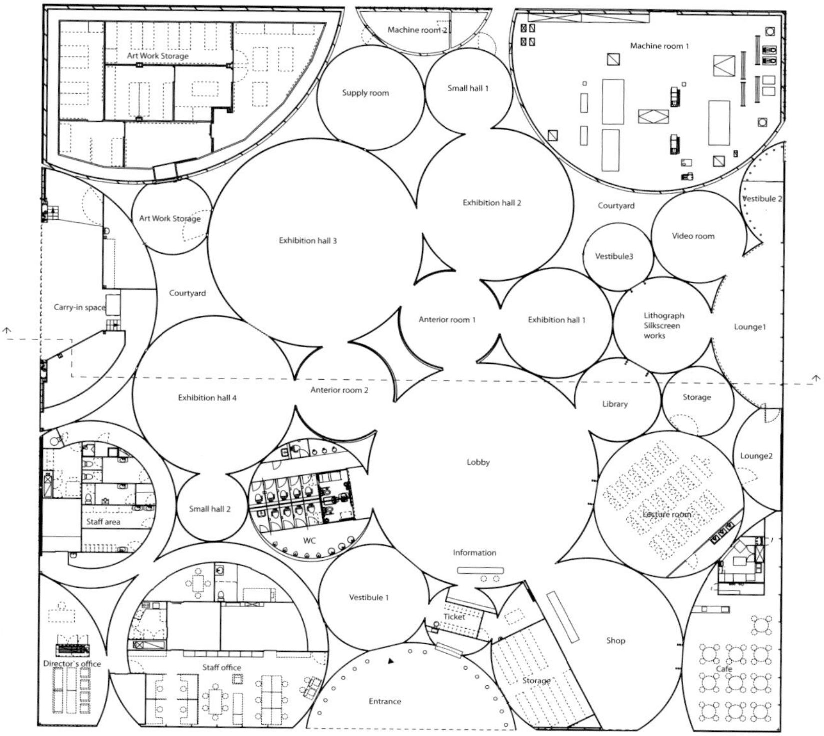

Ground floor plan

Tomihiro Art Museum, situated a couple of hours' drive from Tokyo, overlooks a man-made lake. The museum pays tribute to the work of a well-known athlete, Tomihiro Hoshino, who became a watercolour artist after he was paralysed from the neck down

11/2012

2c